death at an early age

Jonathan Kozol

The Destruction of the Hearts and Minds of
Negro Children in the Boston Public Schools

A NATIONAL GENERAL COMPANY

DEATH AT AN EARLY AGE

*A Bantam Book / published by arrangement with
Houghton Mifflin Company*

PRINTING HISTORY

Houghton Mifflin edition published October 1967

2nd printing ..... October 1967	4th printing ..... October 1967
3rd printing ..... October 1967	5th printing ..... October 1967

Portions of this book have appeared in
THE ATLANTIC *and* THE HARVARD EDUCATIONAL REVIEW

Serialized in THE BOSTON GLOBE *October 1967
and excerpted in* THE PROGRESSIVE *November 1967*

Book-of-the-Month Club edition published March 1968

Bantam edition published May 1968

2nd printing .... May 1968	7th printing ...... March 1969
3rd printing .... May 1968	8th printing .... May 1969
4th printing .... June 1968	9th printing ..... August 1969
5th printing ..... August 1968	10th printing ...... March 1970
6th printing ... September 1968	11th printing .... June 1970

12th printing ... September 1970

13th printing

14th printing

15th printing

Bantam Books are published by Bantam Books, Inc., a National
General company. Its trade-mark, consisting of the words "Bantam
Books" and the portrayal of a bantam, is registered in the United
States Patent Office and in other countries. Marca Registrada.
Bantam Books, Inc., 666 Fifth Avenue, New York, N.Y. 10019.

PRINTED IN THE UNITED STATES OF AMERICA

JONATHAN KOZOL'S
COURAGEOUS BESTSELLER
DEATH AT AN EARLY AGE

"THE HEARTBREAKING STORY IT TELLS HAS TO BE READ . . . I hope some of those Congressmen who are now looking into the causes of riots will find time to read this honest and terrifying book . . . Mr. Kozol charges the Boston School Committee and the system they run with spiritual and psychological murder. Nothing in what they say, some of it supplied word for word in the book's notes, makes the accusation seem excessive."

The New York Times

"It is simple, lucid, horrifying . . . Mr. Kozol has written a very disturbing book. He is writing of the Boston Public School system, but he could be writing of the system in almost any city in the country."

Christian Science Monitor

This Book Is
Dedicated
To Ellen Jackson

Some day, maybe, there will exist a well-informed, well-considered, and yet fervent public conviction that the most deadly of all possible sins is the mutilation of a child's spirit; for such mutilation undercuts the life principle of trust, without which every human act, may it feel ever so good and seem ever so right, is prone to perversion by destructive forms of conscientiousness.

ERIK ERIKSON

PREFACE

I HOPE some of those Congressmen who are now looking into the causes of riots will find time to read this
honest and terrifying book by Jonathan Kozol, a young
teacher fired from his job by the Boston school system
for using a poem by Langston Hughes that was not on
the prescribed list of "reading materials." Mr. Kozol
may even be called to Washington, and asked to tell
our Congressmen what he experienced in an awful,
hellish struggle, waged—of all places—in a city that
fancies itself "the cradle of liberty," and dotes on its
illustrious past. If he testified, perhaps the gentle,
earnest, thoughtful quality of his mind, so apparent in
this book, might be caught by the same television cameras that usually bring us our daily quota of evasive,
pointless rhetoric from "important" people.

"Death at an Early Age" is not a long book. Its content can be easily summarized, but the heartbreaking
story that it tells has to be read, and cannot be dis-
tilled into a review. Mr. Kozol entered the Boston
schools as a substitute teacher in 1964, and the next
spring he was summarily dismissed. Very simply, his
book tells what happened in between, to him as a
teacher and to the children, mostly Negro, he tried so
hard to help and befriend. What emerges is an unspar-
ing picture of American education as it exists today in
the ghettos of our major Northern cities. Perhaps the
United States Information Agency will not want to use
the book abroad.

Right off, Mr. Kozol found himself torn, confused
and appalled. His "classroom" was the corner of an

auditorium in which other classes were also held. In
that same building children sat in a "dank and dirty
urine-smelling cellar." One day a large window fell in
as Mr. Kozol tried to teach his class. Not only was the
school a disgraceful hovel—overcrowded, understaffed,
something out of a Dickens novel—but the city did not
provide police for the children who had to cross dangerous streets to reach the building, though once inside the teachers made sure no boy or girl felt at loose
ends or unwatched.

In point of fact, the children were relentlessly and
at times brutally tyrannized, and the major portion of
this book documents exactly how. The rattan is used.
The author describes the welts he saw, and even the
serious injury one child sustained. All day long the
children learn rules and regulations—to the point that
whatever is original in them, whatever is *theirs* by
virtue of experience or fantasy, becomes steadily discouraged and denied. What is even more awful to con-
template, boys and girls are taught by men and women
who refer to Negroes as "black stuff" and worse.

The reader will find out about the cynicism, condescension, outright racism, and severely anti-intellec-
tual attitudes that Mr. Kozol quite easily and openly
encountered as a teacher among teachers. The city of
Boston may someday (when is anyone's guess) tear
down its already crumbling school buildings and provide its poor children with the best imaginable "facilities" and "materials." But it is quite another question
whether any American city is ready to look into its
own soul, and admit to the subtleties of hate and terror
that persist in the disguise of "education" or "law-
enforcement."

The finest moments in this book are those in which
the author quite openly examines his own, ordinary
("normal," if you will) willingness to go along with
the rest, to submit to the very mean and stupid practices he so clearly recognized. Teachers in Boston and

elsewhere may find him harsh on the "profession," but
he does not spare himself, either.

Like the rest of us, he can excuse and condone—or
simply ignore—events that threaten his "standing," his
job, his yearly income, his day-to-day relationship with
his peers. Like us he is capable of justifying the unjustifiable, or at least denying his own obligation to
oppose what can easily be considered an impossible
situation. There are moments in this life when to do
the practical or wise thing is, in fact, to take the most
corrupt and hurtful course possible. Mr. Kozol lets
us see how those moments fall upon all of us—the
would-be friends and supporters of what is "good"
and "right," and of course "professional."

Eventually—inevitably we only now know—Jonathan
Kozol slipped and brought down upon himself the self-
righteous wrath of what emerges in his book as a
hopelessly insensitive bureaucracy. The charges lev-
eled against him were absurd: he taught Langston
Hughes and Robert Frost to Negro children; he
showed them pictures by Paul Klee, and read to them
from Yeats—with surprising responses from his "disadvantaged" class.

Like so many of us, he can move on, obtain another
job—and write this book. What of the children he describes, and their cousins and parents and neighbors?
At the end of this book we are taken to a meeting of
the Boston School Committee, to meet up with the
vulgar, tricky and abusive comments of those "leaders"
who control and direct the education of thousands of
American children.

In the strongly worded title he has given his book,
Mr. Kozol charges the Boston School Committee and
the system they run with spiritual and psychological
murder. Nothing in what they say, some of it supplied
word for word in the book's notes, makes the accusation seem excessive.

                                    —ROBERT COLES

TO THE READER

WITH the exception of certain named public figures, characters in this book do not have counterparts in real life. Aspects of teaching hierarchies, grade levels, teacher positions and concomitant details within the schools described are also presented in a manner which will not identify real people. Nevertheless, important attitudes, character traits, acts or stated viewpoints ascribed to faculty, administration and pupils in this book accurately reflect the author's experience in the Boston Public Schools.

FOREWORD

DURING the academic year 1964-1965, I found myself teaching in a segregated classroom of the Boston Public Schools. With no training in education and no experience as a teacher, I was sent into an overcrowded ghetto school on a substitute basis, given a year-long assignment, though on a day-to-day salary, to teach a Fourth Grade class within a compensatory program that had been designed for Negro children and that was intended to preserve the racial status quo in Boston by upgrading the segregated schools.

Disheartened by conditions in my school building, and being an habitual note-taker, I soon began to amass a large number of envelopes of handwritten notes. By habit, I held onto these notes and, on a free weekend during the middle of the winter, I made a first attempt at putting them together into some sort of shape and sequence. The first outgrowth of this effort was an essay of about thirty-five pages, which I wrote for my own sense of relief and clarification and then set aside, feeling that it had already served its purpose and thinking it of no further use.

In March, however, I showed this writing to a friend of mine, Faith Morrow, who suggested that the essay seemed to her to be the beginning of a book. I did not think of it again, but continued making jottings and putting them in order and then, at some point in the early summer, after the unexpected events which will be described here had subsided, I began for the first time to see the overall outline of this book.

Since that first summer of 1965, and in the course

of several revisions, the manuscript has been read in detail by a large number of critics and teachers, scholars and friends.

Noel Day was the first person to read this manuscript for me and he did it kindly at a time when it was twice its present length. His enthusiasm for the project encouraged me to keep on with it and his criticism enabled me to see some of the problems and to decide what should be done.

In the intervening months, the book has profited from the judgment and opinion of a number of other people closely involved with Boston and with education. Among these I would like to mention especially Arthur Gartland, Robert Levey, Diane Divoky, Ronald Kessler, Melvin Maddocks, Robert Coles, Tim Leland, Mark Mirsky, Nancy Verre, Donald White, Charles Reed, John Katz and Herbert Kohl. In its final revision, it was read in particular detail by William Barclay, Laurence Langer, Annette Holman, Phyllis Ryan and Lewis Weinstein, all of whom helped me greatly, as well as by my mother and father, who cut into their own crowded schedules to offer final emendations to the book.

Throughout this time I have been fortunate enough to have received legal advice from several people held in the highest regard in this community. For general advice about my position in the Boston school system, I am indebted to Calvin Bartlett and to the late Mark De Wolfe Howe. For specific advice about matters related to this book, I am indebted to Gerald Berlin.

I have also received steady encouragement and advice from many of the parents and community workers in Roxbury. For reasons of confidence, as well as of numbers, I am not able to name all of these people. I would, however, like to give special thanks to John and Julia Walker, Margaret Fortes, Joyce Johnson, Thelma Burns, Bert and Eloise Barros, Bessie Washington, Ella Wornum, Yvonne Ruelas, Eric and Evadney Powell, Mildred Whitley, Ella White, Evelyn Richardson, Bob Phillips, Evelyn Cobb, Betty Terry, Jean McGuire, Carrie Turnbow, Elizabeth Johnson, Gordon Brumm, Don and Peter Halfkenny, Lee Daniels and Joyce Grant. Few of these people were aware of the writing of this book, but all of them, by their loyalty and friendship, helped to make it possible.

Finally, and more than to anyone else, I would like to offer thanks and acknowledge gratitude to Rebecca Morriss—a woman who cared about Stephen and Frederick in the same way that she cares about her own young child, who believes in integration and in the miracle of good education, and who has given of herself unrelentingly, and with deep commitment, in the dream and belief that these things will some day come to be.

To all of these people, and to the hundreds of young schoolchildren who have inspired my life with energy and value throughout these three years, I offer my deep thanks.

ONE

STEPHEN is eight years old. A picture of him standing in front of the bulletin board on Arab bedouins shows a little light-brown person staring with unusual concentration at a chosen spot upon the floor. Stephen is tiny, desperate, unwell. Sometimes he talks to himself. He moves his mouth as if he were talking. At other times he laughs out loud in class for no apparent reason. He is also an indescribably mild and unmalicious child. He cannot do any of his school work very well. His math and reading are poor. In Third Grade he was in a class that had substitute teachers much of the year. Most of the year before that, he had a row of substitute teachers too. He is in the Fourth Grade now but his work is barely at the level of the Second. Nobody has complained about the things that have happened to Stephen because he does not have any mother or father. Stephen is a ward of the State of Massachusetts and, as such, he has been placed in the home of some very poor people who do not want him now that he is not a baby any more. The money that they are given for him to pay his expenses every week does not cover the other kind of expense—the more important kind which is the immense emotional burden that is continually at stake. Stephen often comes into school badly beaten. If I ask him about it, he is apt to deny it because he does not want us to know first-hand what a miserable time he has. Like many children, and many adults too, Stephen is far more concerned with hiding his abased condition from the view of the world than he is with escaping that condition. He lied to me first when I asked him how his eye got so battered. He said it happened from being hit by accident when somebody opened up the door. Later, because it was so bruised and because I questioned him, he admitted that it was his foster mother who had flung him out onto the porch. His eye had struck the banister and it had closed and purpled. The children in the class were frightened to see him. I thought that they also felt some real compassion, but perhaps it was just shock.

Although Stephen did poorly in his school work, there was one thing he could do well. He was a fine artist. He made delightful drawings. The thing about them that was good, however, was also the thing that got him into trouble. For they were not neat and orderly and organized but entirely random and casual, messy, somewhat unpredictable, seldom according to the instructions he had been given, and—in short—real drawings. For these drawings, Stephen received considerable embarrassment at the hands of the Art Teacher. This person was a lady no longer very young who had some rather fixed values and opinions about children and about teaching. Above all, her manner was marked by unusual confidence. She seldom would merely walk into our class but seemed always to sweep into it. Even for myself, her advent, at least in the beginning of the year, used to cause a wave of anxiety. For she came into our class generally in a mood of self-assurance and of almost punitive restlessness which never made one confident but which generally made me wonder what I had done wrong. In dealing with Stephen, I thought she could be quite overwhelming.

The Art Teacher's most common technique for art instruction was to pass out mimeographed designs and then to have the pupils fill them in according to a dictated or suggested color plan. An alternate approach was to stick up on the wall or on the blackboard some of the drawings on a particular subject

that had been done in the previous years by predominantly white classes. These drawings, neat and
ordered and very uniform, would be the models for
our children. The art lesson, in effect, would be to
copy what had been done before, and the neatest
and most accurate reproductions of the original
drawings would be the ones that would win the
highest approval from the teacher. None of the new
drawings, the Art Teacher would tell me frequently,
was comparable to the work that had been done in
former times, but at least the children in the class
could try to copy good examples. The fact that they
were being asked to copy something in which they
could not believe because it was not of them and did
not in any way correspond to their own interests did
not occur to the Art Teacher, or if it did occur she
did not say it. Like a number of other teachers at my
school and in other schools of the same nature, she
possessed a remarkable self-defense apparatus, and
anything that seriously threatened to disturb her point
of view could be effectively denied.

How did a pupil like Stephen react to a teacher of
this sort? Alone almost out of the entire class, I think
that he absolutely turned off his signals while she was
speaking and withdrew to his own private spot. At
his desk he would sit silently while the Art Teacher
was talking and performing. With a pencil, frequently
stubby and end-bitten, he would scribble and fiddle and
cock his head and whisper to himself throughout the
time that the Art Teacher was going on. At length,
when the art lesson officially began, he would perhaps
push aside his little drawing and try the paint and
paper that he had been given, usually using the
watercolors freely and the paintbrush sloppily and a
little bit defiantly and he would come up with things
that certainly were delightful and personal and private, and full of his own nature.

If Stephen began to fiddle around during a lesson,
the Art Teacher generally would not notice him at

first. When she did, both he and I and the children around him would prepare for trouble. For she would go at his desk with something truly like a vengeance and would shriek at him in a way that carried terror. "Give me that! Your paints are all muddy! You've made it a mess. Look at what he's done! He's mixed up the colors! I don't know why we waste good paper on this child!" Then: "Garbage! Junk! He gives me garbage and junk! And garbage is one thing I will not have." Now I thought that that garbage and junk was very nearly the only real artwork in the class. I do not know very much about painting, but I know enough to know that the Art Teacher did not know much about it either and that, furthermore, she did not know or care anything at all about the way in which you can destroy a human being. Stephen, in many ways already dying, died a second and third and fourth and final death before her anger.

Sometimes when the Art Teacher was not present in our classroom, and when no other supervisory person happened to be there, Stephen would sneak up to me, maybe while I was sitting at my desk and going over records or totaling up the milk money or checking a paper, so that I would not see him until he was beside me. Then, hastily, secretly, with mystery, with fun, with something out of a spy movie, he would hand me one of his small drawings. The ones I liked the most, to be honest, were often not completely his own, but pictures which he had copied out of comic books and then elaborated, amended, fiddled with, and frequently added to by putting under them some kind of mock announcement ("I AM THE GREAT-EST AND THE STRONGEST") which might have been something he had wished. I think he must have seen something special and valuable about comic books, because another thing that he sometimes did was just cut out part of a comic book story that he liked and bring it in to me as a present. When he did this, as with his paintings and drawings, he usually would belittle his gift by crumpling it up or folding it up very tiny before he handed it to me. It was a way, perhaps, of saying that he didn't value it too much (although it was clear that he did value it a great deal) in case I didn't like it.

If the Art Teacher came upon us while he was slipping me a picture he had drawn, both he and I were apt to get an effective lashing out. Although she could be as affectionate and benevolent as she liked with other children, with Stephen she was almost always scathing in her comments and made no attempt at seeming mild. "He wants to show you his little scribbles because he wants to use you and your affection for him and make you pity him but we don't have time for that. Keep him away. If you don't, I'll do it. I don't want him getting near you during class."

For weeks after that outburst, when we had been caught in the act of friendship, he stopped coming near me. He stopped bringing me his drawings. He kept to his seat and giggled, mumbled, fiddled. Possibly he felt that he was doing this for my sake in order not to get me into further trouble. Then one day for a brief second he got up his nerve and darted forward. He crumpled up some paper in his fist and handed it to me quickly and got back into his chair. The crumpled paper turned out to be more funnies that he had painstakingly cut out. Another time he dropped a ball of crunched-up math paper on my desk. On the paper he had written out his age—eight years old—and his birthday—which I seem to remember came at Christmas. I also remember that once he either whispered to me or wrote to me on a note that he weighed sixty pounds. This information, I thought, came almost a little boastfully, even though it obviously isn't a lot to weigh if you are almost nine, and I wondered about it for a time until it occurred to me that maybe it was just one of very few things that he knew about himself, one of the half dozen measurable facts that had anything to do with him in the world, and so—like all people, using as best they can whatever they've got—he had to make the most of it.

I think that much of his life, inwardly and outwardly, must have involved a steady and, as it turned out, inwardly at least, a losing battle to survive. He battled for his existence and, like many defenseless humans, he had to use whatever odd little weapons came to hand. Acting up at school was part of it. He was granted so little attention that he must have panicked repeatedly about the possibility that, with a few slight mistakes, he might simply stop existing or being seen at all. I imagine this is one reason why he seemed so often to invite or court a tongue-lashing or a whipping. Doing anything at all that would make a teacher mad at him, scream at him, strike at him, would also have been a kind of ratification, even if it was painful, that he actually was there. Other times, outside of school, he might do things like pulling a fire alarm lever and then having the satisfaction of hearing the sirens and seeing the fire engines and knowing that it was all of his own doing and to his own credit, so that at least he would have proof in that way that his hands and his arm muscles and his mischievous imagination actually did count for something measurable in the world. Maybe the only way in which he could ever impinge upon other people's lives was by infuriating them, but that at least was something. It was better than not having any use at all.

I remember that the Art Teacher once caught him out in the back, in the hallway, in front of a big floor-length coat-closet mirror. She grabbed him by the arm and pulled him into the classroom and announced to me and to the children in the classroom that he was "just standing there and making faces at himself and staring." While she talked, he looked away and examined the floor with his eyes, as he did so often, because he was embarrassed by being exposed like that. I thought it was needlessly cruel of her to have hauled him before the children in that manner, and surely a little hesitation on her part might have given her a moment to think why he might *like* to see himself in a mirror, even if it was only to see a scratched reflection. I didn't think it was shameful for him to be doing that, even to be making funny faces. It seemed rather normal and explicable to me that he might want to check up on his existence. Possibly it was a desperate act, and certainly a curious one, but I do not think it was unnatural. What did seem to me to be unnatural was the unusual virulence of the Art Teacher's reaction.

Another time, seeing him all curled up in one of the corners, I went over to him and tried to get him to look up at me and smile and talk. He would not do that. He remained all shriveled up there and he would not cry and would not laugh. I said to him: "Stephen, if you curl up like that and will not even look up at me, it will just seem as if you wanted to make me think you were a little rat." He looked down at himself hurriedly and then he looked up at me and he chuckled grotesquely and he said, with a pitiful little laugh: "I *know* I couldn't be a rat, Mr. Kozol, because a rat has got to have a little tail!" I never forgot that and I told it later to a child psychiatrist, whose answer to me made it more explicit and more clear: "It is the absence of a tail which convinces him that he has not yet become a rat." Perhaps that is overly absolute and smacks a bit of the psychiatric dogmatism that seems so difficult to accept because it leaves so little room for uncertainty or doubt; yet in this one instance I do not really think that it carries the point too far. For it is the Boston schoolteachers themselves who for years have been speaking of the Negro children in their charge as "animals" and the school building that houses them as "a zoo." And it is well known by now how commonly the injustices and depredations of the Boston school system have compelled its Negro pupils to regard themselves with something less than the dignity and respect of human beings. The toll that this took was probably greater upon Stephen than it might have been upon some other children. But the price that it exacted was paid ultimately by every child, and in the long run I am convinced that the same price has been paid by every teacher too.

TWO

MANY people in Boston are surprised, even to this day, to be told that children are beaten with thin bamboo whips within the cellars of our public schools and that they are whipped at times for no greater offense than for failing to show respect to the very same teachers who have been describing them as niggers. Some rules exist about these whippings and a number of public statements have been made by the school administration in their defense. Some of the rules and some of the public statements are in themselves revelatory of the attitudes which still prevail within the system. One of the present School Committee members, Mr. Thomas Eisenstadt, has made the following remarks in regard to the use of the rattan: "The conditions . . . under which it may be employed are very explicit; for example, a written report must be made and kept on file in the principal's office stating the reason for using the rattan. Also a witness must be present when the rattan is administered, and the name of the said witness must be recorded in the principal's report. Since I have been a member of the School Committee, and that has been over three and one-half years, not one instance of abuse of this prerogative by a teacher or by anyone else has been brought to my attention. The rattan is used conservatively and not indiscriminately." *

* For this, and for all subsequently quoted material from public figures, as well as for all factual matters of public record, references are given beginning on page 237.

Another statement on the subject is that given to a Boston newspaper by Miss Marguerite Sullivan, until recently the Deputy Superintendent for elementary schools in Boston. "She noted that the extent of the rattanning is usually limited to three blows on the hand: 'And the child is never held by the teacher. If he won't put out his hand, the matter is taken up with the parents.'"

The Boston Teachers' Handbook also contains these rules: "Corporal punishment shall not be inflicted when it might aggravate an existing physical impairment or produce or threaten to produce permanent or lasting injury . . . Violent shaking or other gross indignities are expressly forbidden. Cases of corporal punishment shall be reported by each teacher on the dates of their occurrence in writing . . . These reports shall state the name of the pupil, the name of the witness, the amount of punishment, and the reason therefor . . ."

These stipulations are daydreams to anyone who knows certain of the Boston schools. Whippings were frequently given at my school without a witness present. Cards were commonly not filed, if for no other reason than that this task alone would have taken some of the teachers several hours. Students were repeatedly grabbed, shaken and insulted. Parents were rarely notified. And at least one child in my school was whipped in such a way as to leave on his hand a physical impairment in the form of a large raised scar which may be with him all his life. I know this boy well, for he was a student in my room. His name is Frederick. When I first noticed the curious protrusion that rose up near the end of his finger, I asked him about it immediately and he explained it in these words:

"It happened in September before you were my teacher. I was talking and I was sent down to the cellar and when I got the stick I was scared and I must have pulled back my hand a little so I got it on the knuckle instead of on the finger part. I already had a bad infection. They said it was my fault for not keeping my hand still."

It is never simple to accept the idea that these things happen. It came to me that the only conceivable way in which this sort of thing might go unnoticed in a civilized city in the middle of the 1960's would be if the boy had been too terrified to report what had happened to any grown-up outside school, or if that grown-up in turn were too scared to pass it on to anybody else. This was not the case. As Frederick reported it to me, he had indeed told someone. He told his mother. His mother, with whom I have confirmed the remaining details, did not do anything until evening but then became greatly alarmed when she saw the infected knuckle swelling up into the size of a small ball. She took her child to a doctor. Nothing had been exaggerated. The finger was in a highly inflamed state. The boy was not merely treated at City Hospital but it was felt necessary by the doctor that he be put into the hospital for a period that lasted several days. Frederick's medical records afford confirmation of this injury although of course the records do not make any mention of the whipping.

When I spoke to Frederick's mother, I asked her whether she had gone up to school to demand an explanation. She told me that she had but that she had not gotten further than the Art Teacher. Frederick had been in art class at the time the trouble started; she believed, therefore, that the Art Teacher would be the one to know about it. This turned out to be so. The Art Teacher did know about it. She knew what had happened, and she knew that the boy had been hurt badly and she even knew that he had been subsequently hospitalized, and she did not deny any of it. What she did do, however, was to tell the mother that there was no reason to be angry or to pursue the matter further, for she had, she said, already checked with the male teacher who had given the rattanning and had found out that he had "done the whipping right." I wondered whether she felt this could in any way justify the injury or whether she believed that it could in any way provide exoneration either for herself, as the teacher in charge of the child, or for the man who did the whipping. Because it was done right, according to a rule, did that mean it was permissible? It reminded me of the way that many people in wartime Germany had exonerated themselves for their participation in the deaths of Jewish people on the grounds that what they had done had been done correctly. The truth, of course, in this instance, is that the whipping *hadn't* been done correctly. The rules had not been followed, or else a child with an infected finger would not have been beaten. And possibly the Art Teacher knew this and may have had some doubts about it. For she followed through with an act which suggests that she may have had some later worries. The mother of the child has shown me a handsome card that her son received while he was recuperating from his whipping in the hospital. The card is a get-well card and it is signed with a flourishing hand: *"To Frederick. Get well soon and come back to school again! With Love, from your Art Teacher."* Underneath that, she has signed her name. The envelope bears the address of City Hospital.

It seems to me too simple to call the Art Teacher a blatant hypocrite for sending this message, although the thought occurred to me when I read it. I think that she was no more a hypocrite to send him that card than I was a hypocrite to chat with her in a friendly way day after day after I knew all of these things, or to go out and have a friendly beer and shake hands warmly with the pleasant casual man who did the whipping. All white people, I think, are implicated in these things so long as we participate in America in a normal way and attempt to go on leading normal lives while any one race is being cheated and tormented. But now I believe that we probably will go on leading our normal lives, and will go on participating in our nation in a normal way, unless there comes a time when Negroes can compel us by methods of extraordinary pressure to interrupt our pleasure.

To whip a normal child and scar his finger seems bad enough, but to whip an emotionally disturbed child and to devastate his heart and mind is to go a step further. This happened also in my school building. There were two children to whom it happened in my immediate knowledge. One was Stephen. I don't know how many times he underwent those whippings and I am certain that whatever records exist at school would not be accurate. Unquestionably it happened for a while as often as once every month and probably more often, probably closer to once or twice a week. It happened, I noticed, very often when the class was having math instruction, and this, I came to believe, was closely connected to the nature of the feelings that the Math Teacher at our school tended to show toward kids like Stephen. I ought to explain briefly, although it will become more apparent in the sections that come later, that our school was loaded with a certain number of experts in different subject areas, for art, for math, for reading; and the reason for this was that we were participating in the Boston version of a compensatory education program for Negro children. The compensation involved was of a questionable nature, in fact, and when our city lost the prospect of obtaining two million dollars in federal aid for compensatory education, the reason given was that the federal government just did not consider Boston's program to be providing any kind of legitimate compensation. But even if the program had itself been a wise and splendid one, the experts who arrived on the scene, or who were drafted to serve in it, would have compromised it anyway.

Among the various experts with whom I found that I must deal, and under whose general authority I

worked, were such people as the Art and the Math
and the Reading Teachers. Each of the latter two came
into my classroom for a particular part of every
morning, the Art Teacher twice weekly. During these
periods I was either to observe or else to go out and
do remedial work with other classes. In this way, it
was imagined that a novice teacher would learn from
the old-timers. In the case of the Mathematics
Teacher, in the same way as with the Art Teacher—
although it was somewhat different with the Reading
Teacher—I cannot say that I learned anything at all
except how to suppress and pulverize any sparks of
humanity or independence or originality in children.
What I learned from them specifically of the techniques of teaching I have had to do my best to
unlearn since. The Math Teacher, like the Art
Teacher, did not seem very fond of Stephen. She told
me so freely on more than one occasion. Yet she was
also very much aware of his mental instability and it
was she, rather than I, who was the first to come out
in the open and speak of him as a child who was
not well.

I remember the day that she told me this, snapping
it out with sureness: "The child's not in his right
mind." I asked her, when she said this, if she had
thought of helping him into any kind of treatment.
This was a mistake, however, for it developed that
the Math Teacher was not at all keen about psychiatry.
When I asked about treatment for Stephen, she answered only that she had not thought of it but that,
now that I mentioned it, she was going to have to
admit that she could not go along. When I asked her
why, her answer to me was that "he would just lie
and tell the psychiatrists that we weren't kind to him.
He'd tell them that we were all prejudiced up here."
Within days, Stephen was sent to the cellar for another rattanning and the comment of the Math
Teacher, with no sense of incongruity or injustice,
was, again, that he was "not in his right mind."

Others in the school made similar statements about Stephen. The Assistant Principal, a man who was generally kind and—within the context of this school—relatively enlightened, told me almost exactly the same thing. The man was aware of the situation, as were many people. Nothing was done about it, however, and Stephen continued to get whippings. Nor did I do anything myself. I am afraid that many people may not wish to believe that these were real whippings, or that they honestly scared a child, or that they actually involved substantial pain. If this is the case, then I would like to describe what Stephen was like and how he seemed and behaved when he went downstairs to take his beating.

I have said how little he was. Sixty pounds isn't very heavy. He was skinny, with tiny arms, and he couldn't have been more than four feet tall. He had light-brown skin and a Red Sox baseball jersey. He had terrified tiny little hopeless eyes. He had on corduroy pants, which were baggy. He had on basketball sneakers which looked a few sizes too large. His hair had oil on it and had been shaved down almost to the scalp. He was standing near the men's smoke-room. Up above were the pipes of the cellar ceiling. Nearby was the door to the basement boys' toilet. Out of that doorway urine stank. He looked at the floor. He wouldn't look up. He wouldn't let his eyes depart from one chosen spot. His elbows froze at his sides. The teacher who administered the whipping gave the order to hold out his hands. He wouldn't answer. He was the image of someone in torture. Again the teacher, standing above him, passed down the order. He wouldn't do it. The teacher, now losing his patience, ordered it a third time. And still he wouldn't answer or comply. A fourth time. Yet still this frozen terror. So the decision is made: He will get it twice as many times. The stink still from the toilet. Comment from a passing teacher: "The little bastards don't mind acting up but when it's time for them to take their punishment they suddenly lose all their nerve." He can't hold out forever. And finally he gives in. He breaks down and stops resisting. Hands out. He gets the beating.

The teacher who gives the beating may, in all other instances, seem a decent man. Moreover, even in giving this beating, he may do it absolutely as he is supposed to and in every little detail by the rules. Yet— well done or not, and whatever the man's intent—the tears still come and the welts still are formed upon the light-brown hand. The stick is flexible, light and quick and it must hurt badly or else those winces of screwed-up agony and those tears are an incredibly good act. As for the teacher, in most cases, he behaves with a sense of sobriety. Most teachers do not treat the matter lightly. On the other hand, there are always a couple of teachers (there were some in my school and there are many elsewhere) who will speak about a rattanning in a manner of cynicism and humor and open cruelty and who will not hesitate to intersperse their talk with some pretty straightforward remarks. There are also male teachers who, in the very act of giving a whipping, cannot prevent themselves from manifesting a really unmistakable kind of satisfaction. In my own school and elsewhere I have heard any number of proud and boastful statements about the kind of pain that you can get across.

"When you do it, you want to snap it abruptly or else you are not going to get the kind of effect you want."

"Leave it over-night in vinegar or water if you want it to really sting the hands."

I asked, soon after I had started teaching and observing the acts of other teachers, whether it was within the rules to strike a child or whether that was against the law.

"Don't worry about the law. You just make damn sure that no one's watching."

Other counsel: "Don't let them get too close to you. No matter how you feel. The ones you help the most are the first ones who will axe you in the back."

From a teacher at my school: "The ones I can't stand are the goddamn *little* buggers. The First Graders. And the Second Graders. There's nothing you can do to them—you can't even lift up your goddamn hand."

In special regard to a child like Stephen, one question remains and still poses itself repeatedly: Why would *any* teacher, whatever his bent or inclination, just go ahead and whip a boy whom he knows it will not in any way help or correct for something which that teacher has already acknowledged, both to himself and to others, to be beyond the child's ability to prevent? The beginning of one answer may be found in the fact that segregated schools seem often to require this kind of brutal discipline because of the uneasy feelings which are so often present. The children, enough of them anyway, are quietly smoldering with a generally unimagined awareness of their own degradation. The atmosphere that grows out of this may be one of real danger to the equanimity of a teacher or administrator. I am sure this is one reason at least why discipline comes so fast and so strong and, at times, so unjustly. Possibly, in the case of some of the best teachers, this was the entire story. Thinking of some of the other teachers, however, I am convinced that there was also at times something else happening and once you had seen it in action, and watched it, you would know exactly what it was and would never deny that it was there. You would have to have watched certain people doing it, and to have seen their eyes, to have any idea of what was going on.

"This hurts me," says the old expression, "more than it hurts you." Yet this is said easily and it is just not always so. Sadism has its signs and they are unmistakable. There are moments when the visible glint of gratification becomes undeniable in the white teacher's eyes. Would any teacher be able to say with absolute certainty that he has not sometimes taken pleasure in that slash of the rattan and that he has not felt at times an almost masculine fortification out of the solemnity and quietude and even authoritive control and "decency" with which he struck the child? I have watched a teacher giving the rattan with a look on his face which was certainly the very opposite of abhorrence, and I have heard a teacher speak of it as if it were somehow a physical accomplishment or even some kind of military feat. I am sure that teachers as a class are no more sadistic than any other people, and possibly in this the teachers in Boston are no worse than the teachers anywhere else. But many human beings do take pleasure in inflicting pain on others, and those who have the least to be proud of or to be happy about are often the ones who take that pleasure most.

Sometimes the argument is put forward by white Bostonians that corporal punishment did not begin with Negro children and that it is, in fact, a very old tradition within our public schools. I have never found this a convincing argument. The fact that a crime might have been committed with impunity in the past may make it seem more familiar and less gruesome to certain people but surely it does not give it any greater legality. And the fact that some boys may have been whipped unjustly fifty years ago does not make that injustice more palatable today. Whatever it was once, it just seems wrong in its present context. It does not matter whether it was done once by Yankees to Irish children. And it does not matter, either, if it was done once by Irish to Jews. What does matter is that today it is being used by whites on Negroes and that it is being used in too many cases to act out, on a number of persuasive pretexts, a deeply seated racial hate. If you hear of just any tough teen-ager being beaten on the fingers by his teacher you can assume that a school official someplace is going to be able to pass it off as discipline. But when you hear of a sixty-pound mentally ill Fourth Grader being guarded by two men and whipped by a third for acts that are manifestly crazy, and when the teacher who prepares the punishment is not only gleaming with excitement but has, not ten days before, been speaking calmly of the niggers Down South or the little bastards causing trouble up there in room four, then it seems to me that anyone, including the administrator of such a system, is going to have to admit that something has gone wrong. A School Committee member, as I have shown, has put it into the public record that he has never yet heard of a case of the abuse of corporal punishment in the Boston Public Schools. I think that he and all others who share responsibility for these matters ought to recognize quite clearly that they are hearing of one now.

THREE

I HAVE described already a few of the people who were teaching in my school, but I have not yet really spoken about the teacher who was, in many ways, the most interesting person of all. She was the Reading Teacher. This lady was interesting to me, first of all, because she was one of the most serious and self-consciously moralistic people whom I have ever known. She was also, by all odds, the most effective and most high-powered of the old-fashioned public school teachers who were still around. She was— finally—an extraordinarily, if at times, quite subtly, bigoted woman. At the same time, however, and like many others in America, she considered herself a politically liberal and enlightened person, was shocked by any imputation of prejudiced behavior and even spoke at great length, and sometimes without much mercy, of certain of the dishonesties and secret bigotries of others. She was, I used to feel, not only one of the most complex people in the school, but also the most tragic. Unlike much of the school faculty, this lady was seldom consciously malevolent to anybody. She worked hard, gave many signs of warmth and fondness to various children, and spoke incessantly of her deep feelings for them. She was precisely the sort of person whom an outside observer would instantly describe as "a dedicated teacher," if for no other reason than because she would tell him so. I think it was this last trait—her capacity for overwhelming self-congratulation—which heightened so greatly the sense of irony that surrounded much of her behavior.

I remember a day when she had come up into my classroom during lunchtime. She was in one of her moods of exposing the bigotry of other teachers while at the same time rather pridefully extolling her own virtues. "Others may be prejudiced," she was saying to me. "So and so downstairs uses the word 'nigger.' I know I've heard him say it with my own ears. It makes me sick every time I hear him say that. If a person feels that way I don't know what he's doing teaching at this school. You wouldn't imagine the kinds of things I used to hear . . . Last year there was a teacher in this school who used to call them 'black stuff.' Can you imagine somebody even thinking up a phrase like that? If people are prejudiced they should not be teaching here."

Another time, she spoke of the same matter in these words: "Others may be prejudiced. I know that I am not. There are hundreds like me. Thank God for that. Some teachers are prejudiced. The majority are not. We are living in a time when everything is changing. Things are going along but they must not change too fast."

I remember that I felt astonished at her certainty. I told her, for my own part, that I would feel very uneasy making that kind of statement. I said that on many occasions I had become convinced that my thinking was prejudiced, sometimes in obvious ways and sometimes in ways that lay deeper and would not have been so easy for other people to observe. Furthermore, I said, I also was convinced that I was prejudiced at a level of depth, and in a manner hardened over so many years, that some of that prejudice undoubtedly would always be within me.

"Well I'm not," she replied to me with much emotion.

I did not try to turn any accusation toward her. Everything I said was directed at "people in general," at "white society," and mainly at myself. I said to the Reading Teacher that, so far as my own feelings

were concerned, I had no doubt of what I was saying.
I had learned, in some of the work I'd done in Roxbury—certainly in much of the work I'd done for
CORE—that more than once I must have hurt somebody's feelings badly by an undercurrent or an unconscious innuendo in my talk or else the people
I was talking to just would not have winced the way
they had. I said I was certain, from any number of
similar moments that there was plenty of regular
old-time prejudice in me, just as in almost every other
white man I ever saw.

To this, however, the Reading Teacher snapped
back at me again, and now with an absolute self-
confidence: "In me there is none."

We stood together in the doorway. The children sat
in their chairs. It was almost the end of lunchtime.
Each child was having his milk except the ones who
couldn't afford it. Sometimes white and Negro children chattered with each other, and it was normal
and natural and pleasant to watch that, but there
were not sufficient white children for it really to
happen freely enough. There were not enough children who were not black. The Reading Teacher
looked out at the children and she said to me, from
where we were standing: "Roger over there, I think,
is the most unhappy child in this class." Roger was
one of only three white boys in my class. He was
sitting behind Stephen. She did not see Stephen sitting in front of him. She said to me: "When I look
at them I do not see white or black." I listened to
her and looked at her and thought about what she
was saying. She said, "I do not see white or black."
But I felt really that she saw white much more
clearly than she saw black. She saw the quiet and
unhappy little white boy. She did not see Stephen
before him, his hands all welted and his face all
scarred with scabs. "I see no color difference," she
told me. "I see children in front of me, not children
who are black. It has never made a difference to me.
White skin or black skin, they all are made by God."

One day when we talked about it, she told me about a trip she had made to Europe the summer before. She told me that a man on the boat, during the evening, had come across the floor to dance with her. But the man's skin was black. "I knew it was wrong but I honestly could not make myself say yes to that man. It was because he was a Negro. I just could not see myself dancing with that man."

I didn't know if anyone could be condemned for being honest. "What if I fell in love with a Negro girl?" I asked her.

She told me the truth: "I would be shocked."

I said I didn't see why she couldn't dance with a Negro passenger.

"I could not do it."

She also said, "If you married a Negro girl I have to admit that I would feel terribly sad."

I did not have that in my mind, but about what she had been saying I found I was still puzzled. "Would you have Negroes come and visit you or come and have dinner with you in the evening?"

And to that the answer was clear and elucidating and exact: "They could come and visit if I invited them to come but not as you could come to see me. They could not feel free to just drop in on me. I would have to draw the line at that."

Hearing that, I asked myself what this kind of feeling meant in terms of one teacher and one child. This woman had drawn the line "at that" just as the city had drawn the line of the ghetto. A Negro was acceptable, even lovable, if he came out only when invited and at other times stayed back. What did it do to a Negro student when he recognized that his teacher felt that she had to "draw the line at that"? Did it make him feel grateful for the few scraps that he got or did it make him feel bewildered instead that there ought to be any line at all? The Reading Teacher apparently was confident that the line did not descend, in her feelings, to the level of the children—or that, if it did, it would not be detected by them. I gained the impression, on the contrary, that that line was very much in evidence in the classroom and that many of the children were aware of it.

There were two ways in which I thought the Reading Teacher would unknowingly but consistently reveal the existence of that line. One of them, certainly the less important, was in the occasional favors that she showed and in the kinds of arrangements that she would make for various children. To one of my pupils I remember that she brought in and gave as a present a really fine and expensive children's book. I recall that she brought it in and handed it to the child in full view of the class and spoke of how much the little girl deserved it and of how warmly she admired her. For another child, she did something different. He was a poor boy from a large family and so she tried to arrange a stay for him at summer camp. In the case of a third child, she made a friendly contact with his parents, invited them on a couple of occasions to come over and visit in her home, and in general took a warm and decent interest in his up-bringing. The point of this is that all three of these children were white and, while all may well have deserved her help or fondness (and it is hard to imagine what child would not), nonetheless it is striking that the white children in our school were in a very definite and dwindling minority and, during the course of the entire year in which I was teaching, I did not once observe her having offered to do anything of that sort for any child who was Negro, unless it was prompted by a stark emergency. I could not help noticing as well that when I took it on my own initiative to do something similar for a couple of the Negro children in my class, she heard about it immediately and came up to advise me that it was not at all a good idea.

In November I began giving Frederick a lift home after class, for he lived only about three blocks from the school. In December I also started to make occasional visits to see Stephen on the weekends and finally one day I took him over to Harvard to visit at the Peabody Museum. On Christmas Eve I brought him some crayons and some art paper and visited for a while in his home. From all of these trivial actions, but especially from the last, I was seriously discouraged. It was not good practice, it was not in accord with teaching standards, it could not help but ruin discipline if a teacher got to know a pupil outside class. Yet the person who offered me this criticism had just done many things of a similar nature for a number of white children. It seemed evident to me, as it must by now be evident also to her, that the rule or the standard or the policy or the pattern that dictates a separation between a teacher and his pupil was being understood at our school, and was being explicitly interpreted, in precisely such a way as to maintain a line of color. The rule was there. It was relaxed for white children. It was enforced rigorously for Negroes. In this way the color line grew firm and strong.

There was another way in which the Reading Teacher showed her preference. It was in the matter of expectations: of what you could even hope to look for "in these kinds of children," meaning children who were Negro. Directly hooked onto this, often expressed in the same sentence, was a long and hard-dying panegyric for the past. The last, the panegyric, was one of the most common themes and undercurrents in our conversations all year long. Even at moments when she knew it to be inappropriate almost to the point of cruelty, still it was an emotion that she could not contain. Many of the other teachers in the school expressed the same idea frequently, but the most vivid conversations that I remember from the first part of the year were those with the Reading Teacher.

In the early part of winter, I had to ask the Reading Teacher for permission to take my Fourth Grade pupils on a trip to the Museum. I spoke to her of the fact that we would soon be studying Egypt and the desert, and that I thought a morning's visit to the Boston Museum of Fine Arts to see the Egyptian collection and also to wander around and look at some of the paintings would be a good idea. The Reading Teacher's manner of reacting to this request anticipated the way in which she and certain of the other teachers would respond to many other requests that I was to make later in the year. Her first reaction was to turn me down flat. Then, however, she paused for a moment—and, finally, feeling suddenly the need to justify her refusal, added these words:

"With another sort of child, perhaps. The kind of children that we used to have . . ." The moment of panegyric: "Oh we used to do beautiful work here. Wonderful projects! So many wonderful ideas . . ." The present tense again: "Not with these children. You'd take a chance with *him*? or *her*? You'd take a group like them to the museum?"

In a similar vein, I made a suggestion for another child—not for Stephen, because I knew in advance that it would have been doomed to her refusal, but for a little girl. "I thought about next summer. She's one of the best in drawing. I wanted to try to get her into an art class somewhere starting in June."

The Reading Teacher grilled me about it skeptically. "Where?"

I told her I had two places in mind. One was the school that was attached to the Museum. A summer art class for young children was conducted there. Another class that sounded more adventurous was located in Cambridge. The Cambridge program, in a loft-building near Harvard, was being spoken about with much excitement by many of the people interested in art education and it had already won a certain lively reputation for its atmosphere of openness and freedom. The children of some friends of mine were taking classes there.

"How would she get there?"

I answered that I knew someone who would drive her.

"Who'd pay for it?"

I said the same person had offered to pay for the lessons.

The very idea of this little Negro girl bridging the gap between two worlds seemed inconceivable or mechanically unfeasible to the Reading Teacher. To hear her voice you might well have thought it was an arrogant proposal. It was as if a major defiance of chance and nature and of all proper relations and proportions were being suggested. A moment's pause for thinking and then this answer, finally, from the Reading Teacher:

"I wouldn't do anything for Angelina because I just don't like her. But if you're going to do anything, the Museum School's plenty good enough for a child like her."

Because she respected herself as highly as she did, I wonder if the Reading Teacher would have been astonished if somebody had told her that she sounded rather ungentle? Perhaps she would not have been astonished—because she probably would not have believed it. She was one of the most positive persons I have ever known, and she had the most stupendous capacity to convince herself of the justice of her position on almost any issue at all. At any moment when she was reminded, by herself or someone else, that she was being less than Christian or less than charitable to kids who already did not have very much in life, her reaction was apt to be to question whether there was really so much suffering here as people liked to say or whether things were really all that bad. With Stephen, for example, there were only rare moments when she would come face to face with his desperate position. Characteristic of her response to him was the attitude expressed that time when she pointed to the white boy in the seat in back of him and called him the most unhappy child in the class. I remember that when I said to her, "What about Stephen? He doesn't even have parents," the Reading Teacher became instantly defensive and irritated with me and replied: "He has a mother. What are you talking about? He has a foster mother and she is paid by the State to look after his care." But I said maybe it wasn't like having a real mother. And also, I said, the State didn't seem to have time to notice that he was being beaten up by his foster mother while being thoroughly pulverized and obliterated in one way or another almost every day at school. "He has plenty," was her answer. "There are many children who are a great deal worse off. Plenty of white people have had a much harder time than that." Harder than he had? How many? I didn't believe it. Besides, when it got to that point, did it very much matter who, out of many suffering people, was suffering a little bit less or a little bit more? But the Reading Teacher became impatient with the direction of my questioning and she ended it at this point by telling me with finality: "He's getting a whole lot more than he deserves."

It was this, her assumption that people don't deserve a great deal in life, and that a little—even a very, very little for a Negro child—is probably a great deal more than he has earned, which seemed the most disturbing thing about her. And yet at the same time she enjoyed delineating to me the bigotry of others, attacking the Art and Math teachers ruthlessly, when she was not chatting with them, and making hash out of the School Principal when she was not making hash out of someone else. I came into that school as a provisional teacher in October. It was four months, almost the end of February, before I had the courage to begin to speak to her with honesty.

FOUR

THE room in which I taught my Fourth Grade was not a room at all, but the corner of an auditorium. The first time I approached that corner, I noticed only a huge torn stage curtain, a couple of broken windows, a badly listing blackboard and about thirty-five bewildered-looking children, most of whom were Negro. White was overcome in black among them, but white and black together were overcome in chaos. They had desks and a teacher, but they did not really have a class. What they had was about one quarter of the auditorium. Three or four blackboards, two of them broken, made them seem a little bit set apart. Over at the other end of the auditorium there was another Fourth Grade class. Not much was happening at the other side at that minute so that for the moment the noise did not seem so bad. But it became a real nightmare of conflicting noises a little later on. Generally it was not until ten o'clock that the bad crossfire started. By ten-thirty it would have attained such a crescendo that the children in the back rows of my section often couldn't hear my questions and I could not hear their answers. There were no carpetings or sound-absorbers of any kind. The room, being large, and echoing, and wooden, added resonance to every sound. Sometimes the other teacher and I would stagger the lessons in which our classes would have to speak aloud, but this was a makeshift method and it also meant that our classes had to be induced to maintain an unnatural and otherwise unnecessary rule of silence during the rest of the time. We couldn't always do it anyway, and usually the only way out was to try to outshout each other so that both of us often left school hoarse or wheezing. While her class was reciting in unison you could not hear very much in mine. When she was talking alone I could be heard above her but the trouble then was that little bits of her talk got overheard by my class. Suddenly in the middle of our geography you could hear her saying:

"AFTER YOU COMPARE, YOU HAVE GOT TO BRING DOWN."

Or "PLEASE GIVE THAT PENCIL BACK TO HENRIETTA!"

Neither my class nor I could help but be distracted for a moment of sudden curiosity about exactly what was going on. Hours were lost in this way. Yet that was not the worst. More troublesome still was the fact that we did not ever *feel* apart. We were tucked in the corner and anybody who wanted could peek in or walk in or walk past. I never minded an intruder or observer, but to notice and to stare at any casual passer-by grew to be an irresistible temptation for the class. On repeated occasions I had to say to the children: "The class is still going. Let them have their discussion. Let them walk by if they have to. You should still be paying attention over here."

Soon after I came into that auditorium, I discovered that it was not only our two Fourth Grades that were going to have their classes here. We were to share the space also with the glee club, with play rehearsals, special reading, special arithmetic, and also at certain times a Third or Fourth Grade phonics class. I began to make head-counts of numbers of pupils and I started jotting them down:

Seventy children from the two regular Fourth Grades before the invasion.

Then ninety one day with the glee club and remedial arithmetic.

One hundred and seven with the play rehearsal.

One day the sewing class came in with their sewing machines and then that seemed to become a regular practice in the hall. Once I counted one hundred and twenty people. All in the one room. All talking, singing, yelling, laughing, reciting—and all at the same time. Before the Christmas break it became apocalyptic. Not more than one half of the classroom lessons I had planned took place throughout that time.

"Mr. Kozol—I can't hear you."

"Mr. Kozol—what's going on out there?"

"Mr. Kozol—couldn't we sing with them?"

One day something happened to dramatize to me, even more powerfully than anything yet, just what a desperate situation we were really in. What happened was that a window whose frame had rotted was blown right out of its sashes by a strong gust of wind and began to fall into the auditorium, just above my children's heads. I had noticed that window several times before and I had seen that its frame was rotting, but there were so many other things equally rotted or broken in the school building that it didn't occur to me to say anything about it. The feeling I had was that the Principal and custodians and Reading Teacher and other people had been in that building for a long time before me and they must have seen the condition of the windows. If anything could be done, if there were any way to get it corrected, I assumed they would have done it by this time. Thus, by not complaining and by not pointing it out to anyone, in a sense I went along with the rest of them and accepted it as something inevitable. One of the most grim things about teaching in such a school and such a system is that you do not like to be an incessant barb and irritation to everybody else, so you come under a rather strong compulsion to keep quiet. But after you have been quiet for a while there is an equally strong temptation to begin to accept the conditions of your work or of the children's plight as natural. This, in a sense, is what had happened to me during that period and that, I suppose, is why I didn't say anything about the rotting window. Now one day it caved in.

First there was a cracking sound, then a burst of icy air. The next thing I knew, a child was saying: "Mr. Kozol—look at the window!" I turned and looked and saw that it was starting to fall in. It was maybe four or five feet tall and it came straight inward out of its sashes toward the heads of the children. I was standing, by coincidence, only about four or five feet off and was able to catch it with my hand. But the wind was so strong that it nearly blew right out of my hands. A couple of seconds of good luck —for it was a matter of chance that I was standing there—kept glass from the desks of six or seven children and very possibly preserved the original shape of half a dozen of their heads. The ones who had been under the glass were terrified but the thing that I noticed with most wonder was that they tried very hard to hide their fear in order to help me get over my own sense of embarrassment and guilt. I soon realized I was not going to be able to hold the thing up by myself and I was obliged to ask one of the stronger boys in the class to come over and give me a hand. Meanwhile, as the children beneath us shivered with the icy wind and as the two of us now shivered also since it was a day when the mercury was hovering all morning close to freezing, I asked one of the children in the front row to run down and fetch the janitor.

When he asked me what he should tell him, I said: "Tell him the house is falling in." The children laughed. It was the first time I had ever come out and said anything like that when the children could hear me. I am sure my reluctance to speak out like that more often must seem odd to many readers, for at this perspective it seems odd to me as well. Certainly there were plenty of things wrong within that school building and there was enough we could have joked about. The truth, however, is that I did not often talk like that, nor did many of the other teachers, and there was a practical reason for this. Unless you were ready to buck the system utterly, it would become far too difficult to teach in an atmosphere of that kind of honesty. It generally seemed a great deal easier to pretend as well as you could that everything was normal and okay. Some teachers carried out this posture with so much eagerness, in fact, that their defense of the school ended up as something like a hymn of praise and adoration. "You children should thank God and feel blessed with good luck for all you've got. There are so many little children in the world who have been given so much less." The books are junk, the paint peels, the cellar stinks, the teachers call you nigger, and the windows fall in on your heads. "Thank God that you don't live in Russia or Africa! Thank God for all the blessings that you've got!" Once, finally, the day after the window blew in, I said to a friend of mine in the evening after school: "I guess that the building I teach in is not in very good condition." But to state a condition of dilapidation and ugliness and physical danger in words as mild and indirect as those is almost worse than not saying anything at all. I had a hard time with that problem—the problem of being honest and of confronting openly the extent to which I was compromised by going along with things that were abhorrent and by accepting as moderately reasonable or unavoidably troublesome things which, if they were inflicted on children of my own, I would have condemned savagely.

A friend of mine to whom I have confided some of these things has not been able to keep from criticizing me for what he thinks of as a kind of quiet collusion. When I said to him, for example, that the Reading Teacher was trying to do the right thing and that she was a very forceful teacher, he replied to me that from what I had described to him she might have been a very forceful teacher but she was not a good teacher but a very dangerous one and that whether she was *trying* to do the right thing or not did not impress him since what she *did* do was the wrong thing. Other people I know have said the same thing to me about this and I am certain, looking back, that it is only the sheer accident of the unexpected events which took place in my school during the last weeks of the spring that prompted me suddenly to speak out and to take some forthright action. I am also convinced that it is that, and that alone, that has spared me the highly specialized and generally richly deserved contempt which is otherwise reserved by Negro people for their well-intending but inconsistent liberal friends.

After the window blew in on us that time, the janitor finally came up and hammered it shut with nails so that it would not fall in again but also so that it could not open. It was a month before anything was done about the large gap left by a missing pane. Children shivered a few feet away from it. The Principal walked by frequently and saw us. So did supervisors from the School Department. So of course did the various lady experts who traveled all day from room to room within our school. No one can say that dozens of people did not know that children were sitting within the range of freezing air. At last one day the janitor came up with a piece of cardboard or pasteboard and covered over about a quarter of that lower window so that there was no more wind coming in but just that much less sunshine too. I remember wondering what a piece of glass could cost in Boston and I had the idea of going out and buying some and trying to put it in myself. That rectangle of cardboard over our nailed-shut window was not removed for a quarter of the year. When it was removed, it was only because a televison station was going to come and visit in the building and the School Department wanted to make the room look more attractive. But it was winter when the window broke, and the repairs did not take place until the middle of the spring.

In case a reader imagines that my school may have been unusual and that some of the other schools in Roxbury must have been in better shape, I think it's worthwhile to point out that the exact opposite seems to have been the case. The conditions in my school were said by many people to be considerably better than those in several of the other ghetto schools. One of the worst, according to those who made comparisons, was the Endicott, also situated in the Negro neighborhood and, like my own school, heavily imbalanced. At Endicott, I learned, it had become so overcrowded that there were actually some classes in which the number of pupils exceeded the number of desks and in which the extra pupils had to sit in chairs behind the teacher. A child absent one day commonly came back the next day and found someone else sitting at his desk. These facts had been brought out in the newspapers, pretty well documented, and they were not denied by the School Department. Despite this, however, as in most cases like this, nothing had been done. When the parents of the Endicott children pressed the School Department to do something about it, a series of events transpired which told a large part of the story of segregation in a very few words.

The School Department offered, in order to resolve the problem, to buy a deserted forty-year-old Hebrew school and then allot about seven thousand dollars to furnish it with desks and chairs. Aside from the indignity of getting everybody else's castoffs (the Negroes already lived in former Jewish tenements and bought in former Jewish stores), there also was the telling fact that to buy and staff this old Hebrew school with about a dozen teachers was going to cost quite a lot of money and that to send the children down the street a couple of miles to a white school which had space would have saved quite a lot. The

Hebrew school was going to cost over $180,000. To staff it, supply it with books and so forth would cost about $100,000 more. To send the children into available seats in nearby white classrooms (no new teachers needed) would have cost $40,000 to $60,000 for the year. The School Department, it seemed, was willing to spend something in the area of an extra $240,000 in order to put the Negro children into another segregated school. It was hard for me to believe, even after all I had seen and heard, that it could really be worth a quarter of a million dollars to anyone to keep the Negro children separate. As it happened, the School Committee dragged its heels so long and debated the issue in so many directions that most of the school year passed before anything of a final nature was decided. Meanwhile the real children in the real Endicott classrooms had lost another real year from their real lives.

In my own school, there was another bad situation in a Fourth Grade class across the stair-landing. Here in a room in which one window was nailed to the window sill and in which words could not be read clearly on the blackboard because that old blackboard was so scratchy and so worn, there was a gentle soul on the apparent verge of mental breakdown and of whom it was said that he had had a mental collapse not long before. He had been dismissed, I was told, from a previous position in the Boston system after it had grown evident that he could not effectively handle the problems posed by an ordinary crowded class. Instead of being either retired or else given the type of specialized work in which he might have been effective, the man had simply been shunted along into another overcrowded ghetto school. The assignment was unjust both to him and to the children. The classroom to which he had been assigned was filled with chaos, screams and shouting all day long. The man gave his class mixed-up instructions. He was the sort of mild, nervous person who gives instructions in a tone that makes it clear in advance that he does not really expect to be either believed or obeyed. He screamed often but his screams contained generally not force but fear. Bright children got confused; all children grew exhausted. There was very little calm or order. Going in there on an errand during the middle of the morning, it was not always immediately possible to find him. You would not be able to make out where he was in the midst of the movements of the shouting, jumping class. On rare occasions, the children, having no one else to blame for this except their teacher, would rise up in an angry instant and strike back. I remember a day in the middle of January, in quite cold weather, when the teacher went out onto the metal fire escape for a moment for some purpose—perhaps just to regain his composure and try to calm himself down—and one of the children jumped up and slammed the door. It locked behind him. "Let me in!" the man started screaming. It was unjust to him but he must have seemed like Rumpelstiltskin, and the children, not ever having had a chance at revenge before, must have been filled with sudden joy. "Let me in! How dare you," etc. At last they relented. Someone opened up the door and let the man back in.

After I went in there the first time in November, I began to find my attention being drawn repeatedly by two of the children. One of them was a bright and attractive and impatient Negro girl who showed her hatred for school and teacher by sitting all day with a slow and smoldering look of cynical resentment in her eyes. Not only was she bright but she also worked extremely hard, and she seemed to me remarkably sophisticated, even though she was still very much a little child. I thought that she would easily have been the sure candidate for Girls' Latin School or for one of the other local girls' schools of distinction had she not been Negro and not been a victim of this segregated school. For two years now she had had substitute teachers, and this year a permanent teacher in a state of perpetual breakdown. Her eyes, beautiful and sarcastic, told that she understood exactly what was going on. Enough shrewdness and sense of dignity belonged to her that she made no mistake about where to place the blame. She was one of thousands who gave the lie, merely by her silent eloquence, to the utterances of the Boston School Committee. She was a child who, in her insight and calm anger, gave the lie to every myth of a slow and sleepy Negro timidly creeping up and creeping along. Five years from now, if my guess was correct, she would be fourteen and she would be out on picket lines. She would stand there and she would protest because there alone, after so much wasting of her years, would be the one place where her pride and hope would still have a chance. But how could a child like her, with all of her awareness and all of her intelligence, ever in her lifetime find a way to forgive society and the public school system for what it had done to her?

The other child whom I noticed in that Fourth Grade room was in an obvious way less fortunate. In this case it was the situation of a boy who was retarded. For this child, whom I call Edward, there was no chance at all of surviving inwardly within this miserable classroom, still less of figuring out where the blame ought to be applied. The combination of low intelligence with a state of emotional confusion resulted, in him, in behavior which, while never violent, was unmistakably peculiar. No one could have missed it—unless he wanted to, or needed to. The boy walked upstairs on the stairway backward, singing. Many teachers managed not to notice. He walked with his coat pulled up and zippered over his face and inside he roared with laughter, until a teacher grabbed him and slammed him at the wall. Nobody said, "Something is wrong." He hopped like a frog and made frog-noises. Occasionally a teacher would not be able to help himself and would come right out and say, "Jesus, that kid's odd." But I never did hear anyone say that maybe also, in regard to the disposition of this one child at least, something in the system of the school itself was wrong or odd. This was his situation, repeated hundreds of times in other public schools of Boston:

The boy was designated a "special student," categorized in this way because of his measured I.Q. and hence, by the expectation of most teachers, not teachable within a normal crowded room. On the other hand, owing to the overcrowding of the school and the lack of special teachers, there was no room for him in our one special class. Again, because of the school system's unwillingness to bus Negro children into other neighborhoods, he could not attend class in any other school which might have room. The consequence of all of this, as it came down through the channels of the system, was that he was to remain a full year mostly unseen and virtually forgotten, with nothing to do except to vegetate, cause trouble, daydream or just silently decay. He was unwell. His sickness was obvious, and it was impossible to miss it. He laughed to near crying over unimaginable details. If you didn't look closely it seemed often that he was laughing over nothing at all. Sometimes he smiled wonderfully with a look of sheer ecstasy. Usually it was over something tiny: a little dot on his finger or an imaginary bug upon the floor. The boy had a large olive head and very glassy rolling eyes. One day I brought him a book about a little French boy who was followed to school by a red balloon. He sat and swung his head back and forth over it and smiled. More often he was likely to sulk, or whimper or cry. He cried in reading because he could not learn to read. He cried in writing because he could not be taught to write. He cried because he couldn't pronounce words of many syl-

lables. He didn't know his tables. He didn't know
how to subtract. He didn't know how to divide. He
was in this Fourth Grade class, as I kept on thinking,
by an administrative error so huge that it seemed
at times as if it must have been an administrative
joke. The joke of HIM was so obvious it was hard
not to find it funny. The children in the class found
it funny. They laughed at him all day. Sometimes
he laughed with them since it's quite possible, when
we have few choices, to look upon even our own
misery as some kind of desperate joke. Or else he
started to shout. His teacher once turned to me and
said very honestly and openly: "It's just impossible
to teach him." And the truth, of course, in this case,
is that teacher *didn't* teach him; nor had he really
been taught since the day he came into this school.

In November I started doing special work in reading with a number of the slowest readers out of all
of the Fourth Grades. It was not easy to pick them,
for few children at our school read near grade-level.
Only six or seven in my own class were Fourth Grade
readers. Many were at least a year, frequently two
years, behind. Those who had had so many substitutes in the previous two years tended to be in the
worst shape. In selecting this special group of children, it seemed to me that Edward deserved the extra
help as much as anyone. He wanted it too—he made
that apparent. For he came along with excitement
and with a great and optimistic smile and he began
by being attentive to me and appeared happy for
a while. The smiling stopped soon, however, because
he could not follow even the extremely moderate
pace that we were keeping. The other children, backward as they had seemed, were far ahead of him.
He soon began to cry. At this point the Reading
Teacher came rushing on the scene. Her reaction
was not unusual, or unexpected. Rather than getting
angry in any way at all at either the school or the
city or the system for this one child's sake, her anger

was all for him and her outrage and her capacity
for onslaught all came down upon his head. "I will
not have it!" she said of him and of his misery and
then, virtually seething with her decision-making
power, she instructed me that I was not to teach him
any longer. Not taught by me and not by his regular
teacher. I asked her, in that case, by whom he would
be taught from now on, and the answer in effect
was nobody. The real decision, spoken or unspoken,
was that he would not be taught at all. In this, as
in many of the other things I have described, I was
reluctant at that time to argue forcefully. Instead,
I acquiesced in her authority and I quietly did as
I was told. For the duration of the fall and for the
major portion of the winter, the little boy with the
olive smile would ask me, it seemed, almost every
morning: "Mr. Kozol—can I come to reading with
you?" And almost every morning I pretended that
his exclusion was only temporary and I lied to him
and told him: "I'm sorry, Edward. Just not for today."

After a while he got the point that it was permanent.

FIVE

Before I came to teach my Fourth Grade class, I had been a substitute teacher in the Boston school system for four or five weeks. During this period I had a chance to visit several schools and to form some opinion of what was going on in the rest of the city. Of all the schools I saw, the one that seemed most cheerful and hopeful and best kept-up, as well as having the liveliest teachers, was an integrated elementary school not far from the ocean in South Boston. According to the children in the class, of whom about one fourth were Negro, they had very few substitute teachers. The faculty members to whom I spoke confirmed this. The most miserable schools that I saw during this period—most poorly staffed, most grim and most unhappy—were those that were most heavily imbalanced.

In one of these schools, a segregated elementary school in one of the most rundown Negro districts, I received confirmation of the belief that even a modern structure and new equipment could not do away with the problems inherent in a segregated school. The slave-master and black child feeling was prevalent here anyway, and discipline remained the overriding problem. Still children seethed and classes were too crowded and the assignment of substitute teachers was quite common. In the class in which I was placed, a Sixth Grade of almost all black children, I was told by the children that I was the fifth of that many substitutes in that many days. It may have been an exaggeration but I don't see any reason to doubt it for the reason that I've seen exactly the same thing happen in my own school since that time. (Another school, not in the same neighborhood as the one above, but very similar in its racial make-up as it was also in its faculty deficiencies, had twenty-five substitute teachers in one Third Grade class during the three and a half months between September and Christmas of that year.) The children in that Sixth Grade also told me that their regular teacher was a very old lady who was sup-posed to have retired but for some reason had not done so and instead came to school somewhat spo-radically, just about when she felt up to it. While at school she repeatedly nodded off as she sat at her desk and fell asleep. I didn't absolutely believe this until I asked the other teachers, but they assured me it was so. In situations like these, as I since have learned quite clearly, the children have every reason to be truthful and very few reasons to tell lies. It is only the teachers who have at certain times a real stake in lying. Mr. Eisenstadt has said, in conversation with Negro parents, that in a situation of opposing testimonies he would tend to believe the teacher be-cause of course you cannot take the word of the children. My own experience, from one year within this system, would convince me that the exact op-posite is so.

The worst school of all schools in which I ever taught as a substitute teacher was not an ordinary school at all but a "discipline school." I think this was the most depressing place for learning that I have seen anywhere. It was a place for difficult chil-dren, for kids who had been in trouble, for those who had fallen behind, kids who had been arrested, who were truant, who had bad problems, who were disturbed or despairing or unwell. To this school I was sent as a new substitute teacher not only abso-lutely unprepared but also wholly untrained and un-warned. The most curious thing about it is that the

School Department, in asking me to go there, did not even tell me that it was a discipline school but specifically misinformed me when I asked and told me that it was a regular junior high. It was not until I got there that I found out what it was. What it was, was not a school but a dumping ground. It was a dumping ground, I felt, both for undistinguished teachers and for students who had not been manageable or who had not been considered salvageable at more ordinary schools. At this place education seemed to me to have been forgotten, and the Twentieth Century itself seemed to have been forgotten or never seriously encountered. I met a number of the teachers during the time that I was working there, and I remember at least a couple of them clearly.

One was a good-natured and affable person with nothing in particular right or wrong about him except that he seemed to dislike education and had no interest that I could see in kids. He assured me on one of my first days that all revolutions have been begun by intellectuals. I remember that we were out in the schoolyard when he said that and he shoved out his arm in a good imitation of the Hitler salute and he incanted: "Mao Tse-tung! Stalin! Castro! They were all intellectuals. They are the type of people who threaten the free world."

I did not know what I had done to bring that on since I did not walk into that school talking about Stalin or Castro, and the only thing I said that had anything to do with education was that I was thinking of trying to teach some mathematics to my pupils. He also told me that if I was interested in teaching, then I had better get out. "This place isn't a school. It's a zoo. And those are the animals."

When he said it was a zoo, he gestured out to the children in the schoolyard, and the sweep of his hand was terrifying because it seemed to shut out forever all chance of amelioration or education or treatment or any kind of hope. Yet he did not hesitate to talk to me in this way and he seemed assured, for a reason that I did not give to him, that his expressions of contempt for the children would somehow find a willing listener. The same thing has happened to me repeatedly in the Boston school system and it happened in a more dramatic and more damaging way with one of the other teachers at that place.

This man, unlike the first one, was not easygoing and affable at all, although he shared with the first an apparent distaste both for the children and, I thought, for the school. The man was a professional "tough guy" and he had been a marine sergeant before taking the courses and getting the credits to become a teacher. He styled himself very much as a tough guy and seemed to like this designation and the boys accepted it. He told me several tales of his toughness and showed off that toughness out in the schoolyard by throwing a bullet football pass. (I remember that he took a certain amount of relish in trying to "nail" me with a hard one and that I earned the only grains of respect from him I ever had by catching it.) Again he confused me by seeming to like me and for a while he made me feel tied down by his tendency to report to me things that I did not want to hear but which he seemed to feel sure I would enjoy or profit from. It was he, for example, who had given me the advice, that I referred to earlier, of being careful I wasn't observed if I should want to strike a child. He illustrated this warning by relating to me the story of a good friend of his, a teacher in another school, who had struck a boy so hard that the welt marks remained on the child's face for a week and the parents threatened to take the teacher into court. The teacher got out of it, he told me, by using some kind of political connection or some sort of affiliation with the judge. He also managed to get the parents off his back by threatening them with some kind of sordid revelation about their son which he said would have gotten the pupil sent away. So the parents dropped the charge. The point of the lesson, however, was that a teacher could not be too careful. Whack a kid, if you had to, when nobody was looking, but make sure you didn't leave any bruise marks on him. And then just deny it coldly if it ever came to court. When I thought of it later, I was surprised that he had told it to me— because it seemed so damning both to his friend and, in a sense, to him by his seeming to sanction it. Yet it also was a narration which, in a small way, indicated that he knew some people who knew other people who had some connections in the world and so it was a story of which, even in a small way, he could feel proud.

My first two or three days in the discipline school were anything but disciplined or orderly. Few students heard or obeyed me. They wandered in and out of the classroom pretty much at will. (For a time, I did not know how many were my students.) Some of the boys were hostile when I arrived there, and hostile when I left, and never softened or melted for one minute in between. Nonetheless, I did get to be close to several of the boys, and liked many of them, and one day I found myself driving a group home. I did not know at the time that that would be against the rules of the school. One boy, I remember, asked me to leave him at the end of his street. His friend said: "That's because he's embarrassed. He doesn't want you to see what an awful place he lives." Things in the classroom calmed down somewhat after a few days, but the set-up of the place remained miserable for teaching. Two or three of the boys were virtually adult. Others seemed much younger and were reading at the level of the First or Second Grade. I could find no easy books or basic primers in the room. If there were any, no one bothered to tell me where they were or which ones I should be using. Math, I was told, hadn't been taught for a long while and I could believe this when I tried some easy subtraction and division. Few could do either. Some of these boys were of Ninth or Tenth Grade age. With hardly an exception, they seemed disturbed. A large number were Negro. I couldn't single out one who would not, if he weren't poor or weren't colored, have been given some kind of intensive psychiatric aid. As it was, so far as I could find out, they got nothing.

Sometimes a child in a situation like this will recognize, even if it is only distantly, the grotesque nature of the trap that is around him and he will even come out and ask you, pretty straightforwardly, if you will help find the way to escape it. I remember a boy like this at that school who asked me privately, and with much embarrassment, if I would get him a First Grade book at a library or bookstore since he couldn't find such a book at school and was embarrassed at his age to walk into a public place and ask for one. He wanted desperately to read. He knew for sure what he was in for if he could not catch up now. Yet the school offered him nothing and he had to humble himself to plead with me. One of the saddest things on earth is the sight of a young person, already becoming adolescent, who has lost about five years in the chaos and oblivion of a school system and who still not only wants but pleads to learn, as this boy was doing.

The summer before I entered the school system, I had been working as a volunteer tutor in a Roxbury church. About a week after the class started, and after I had been told to admit no more pupils, a boy with the beard of a man appeared, about sixteen or seventeen, who turned out to be the older brother of one of the Fifth Grade pupils in the class. He could have been out playing, earning money, driving a car, doing anything he pleased. Instead he listened outside a volunteer tutor's makeshift class and at the end of each week he would ask me if there was any chance of someone's dropping out so that he could get in to take the empty place. He was in the Eighth Grade but he had never learned to read. People who talk about these things are often heard resorting to the explanation that it "all starts in the home" or else that "these people just don't want to learn." Whenever I hear that, I think of that boy who stood in the hallway outside the door of my classroom for an entire summer of hot and weary mornings, waiting there to walk his sisters home when they were finished and hoping that he might somehow be admitted to the sessions too. There was nothing wrong with his motivation, and there was nothing wrong in his home or home-life either. It was the public schools, pure and simple, which had held him back and made the situation of his life pathetic. It is the same story for thousands of other children all over Boston, and I believe it is the same for children in dozens of other cities in the United States too.

For the slower pupils at the discipline school, as there were so few suitable materials, I found little work to assign other than drawing. I am sure this shows that I lacked much ingenuity but it is the truth that at that point, having been a teacher for about three weeks, I did not have very many ideas about what you could do without materials. While I was working with the others, I would set up subjects for the slower kids to draw. They drew one picture after another. I used to pray that they would take a little longer so that I would have a chance to finish something with the other boys. When they tired of drawing there were mimeographed maps and juvenile pictures to color. The pupils who could read were insulted and bored by the kinds of books that filled the cupboards. There was nothing special, nothing for them, nothing inspired, ingenious, advanced. The only geography book I saw in the classroom was a ten-year-old revision of the same book that I had used as a Seventh Grade pupil a decade and a half before. The principal of the school was an aging, kindly man with little idea of what was going on in the classrooms. He was frail, near retirement, and died of a heart attack that winter. He came up twice, told me where to park my car so I wouldn't get a ticket, and that was as much help as I got. About a third of the school hours were spent at wandering in the schoolyard ("sports"), at shop in the cellar, at cooking (making the lunch), or watching movies. School got out early. One boy in my class howled and cried almost the whole of every day. When he did not howl, a favorite occupation was to lift the flaps of his ancient raincoat (which for some private reason he could never be persuaded to hang up) and run about the classroom, raincoat flying out behind him, only to come to a sudden frozen stop. If I scolded him he would let out a hideous sad groan. Out in the schoolyard another boy spent most of the recess periods posturing as a Hollywood producer, with a "cigarette" (pencil) delicately dangling from his lips.

By the end of a week I recognized that, no matter how hard I tried and no matter how much the children in my class might go along with me, there still was not going to be a real opportunity for me to teach here or for the children to learn. It was not a school. And it wasn't a center for disturbed children. And it wasn't an institution dedicated to salvage. It was a place in which the school system kept its unteachables out of sight and turned them into untouchables. I felt that in almost any other school in the city I would at least have a chance to teach children a few things I knew or could learn. Despite this, I often felt guilty after I left there and I thought that I had ditched the pupils in my room just at the moment when some of them were beginning to feel involved with me. I still don't know whether I should or shouldn't have stayed there or whether, even while I was there, I really was doing any better than dozens of other inexperienced teachers had done before. But I know anyway that my own crisis of conscience in the matter is not the present problem for those boys, nor for anybody else. The problem is the waste of years, the loss of chances, the closing of avenues, the end of hopes which that kind of institution represents. Even if that school should be completely revamped, re-built, re-designed, re-conceived and re-arranged, the guilty burden of the past and of what has already been done to the boys there will remain and it will have been very great.

The line from the boy in my own school who walked backward upstairs, or the child in my own class who talked to himself and got the stick because the city found it cheaper to whip him than to give him any kind of meaningful aid—the path from the many dozens of untaught special students at our school to that full-fledged special school I have been describing is obvious and clear. One of the few things that really work well in the Boston schools is the punitive trip downward. The upward route is ten times harder and more obscure. Punishment is fast but treatment slow. Special helps are hard to come by but bullies are standing by with sticks in their hands at every door. It is not unique. It is not just one school. It is the tone of the entire system. It is the feel of the atmosphere. It is the sense that you cannot do a great many things right but that you can do almost anything wrong. Perhaps in some cases the results of such an attitude will go for weeks or for months or for years before they are fully noticed and detected. Sooner or later, the bitter consequences come out and, when they do, they are apt to have a stunning impact. The problem, however, is that the impact is almost always so short-lived.

In the second week of December in 1965 a very

effective series of articles began to be published in
the pages of the Boston *Globe*. The articles were
written by a young reporter named Robert Levey
and, although I did not have a chance to meet him
until somewhat later, I felt impressed immediately
by the authority of his writing. Many people in the
City of Boston now learned for the first time that
the following things were so:

Sixth Grade children in many of the segregated
schools were "as much as three years behind" the
reading levels of children in some of the other sections of the city. "These same children were average
performers in the second grade, but fell behind more
and more each year . . . The school plant itself is
inadequate and antiquated. The school building program . . . is creeping along at a painfully slow clip.
There are no school libraries in the 175 elementary
and junior high schools. School Dept. records show
Boston students score badly on nationally standardized tests. Students at only three of the city's 16 high
schools score above average as a group. Guidance
and pupil adjustment functions are desperately understaffed. Until last year, just 10 pupil adjustment
counselors covered 17 junior high and 158 elementary schools. That comes to one counselor for every
8,500 students. This staff has been doubled, but it
still leaves each counselor with more than 4,000 students . . ."

Other documentation which I also saw at about
the same time was contained in a booklet known as
the "Interim Report" on racial imbalance of the
State Board of Education. The booklet, published in
the previous summer, presented the findings of a
committee of laymen and various experts set up to
look into the possible existence of racial imbalance
within a number of areas of education but primarily,
as it turned out, within the Boston schools. Printed
on some of the beginning pages of the report were
the names of various persons who were members

of the Board of Education or of the Advisory Committee that had written the document. The names were names of unquestionable distinction in our city: Abram Sachar, President of Brandeis; Asa Knowles, President of Northeastern; Harold Case, President of Boston University; James R. Killian of M.I.T. There were also the names of Erwin D. Canham, editor of the *Christian Science Monitor*; of Ralph Lowell; of Cardinal Cushing; of Boston's widely respected Jewish leader, Lewis Weinstein.

What the Interim Report really achieved was to state in an authoritative manner and from a forum of intense respectability many of the things that people in Roxbury had already been saying now for several years: Boston did have racially imbalanced schools. These schools were, for the most part, inferior. The mere fact of racial imbalance represented a form of inequality. The response by the School Committee to the type of material contained in this report, as well as to the atmosphere of criticism and scrutiny which this and other forms of research and reporting inevitably created, was generally couched in a set of rigid phrases well known by now to the residents of other Northern urban areas. The greatest public attention went consistently to the press statements and pronouncements of the chairman of the School Committee, a lady named Louise Day Hicks. What we had in Boston, Mrs. Hicks would explain, using a term that has since become common in speaking of this issue, were not Negro schools but "neighborhood schools." If it happened to be true that the neighborhoods were Negro, and the schools consequently segregated, well that was unfortunate and perhaps regrettable but it was not the School Committee's business and it was not the School Committee's fault. As for herself, Mrs. Hicks assured the voters that she was not going to stand idly by and look calmly upon the dissolution of a concept so hallowed and so deeply honored as that of the neighborhood school.

Related to this approach was an argument, put forward also by Mrs. Hicks, that Boston schools could not be segregated in any case because we had a system in our city that was known as "Open Enrollment." This meant that students had the theoretical right to go to any school they wished. Boston, said Mrs. Hicks, was "unique in that any student can go to any public school in the city, provided that there is space available and the parents will pay transportation costs." Looking at the second proviso, we can see that the position was a cruel one, insincere and hardly tenable. For a theoretical right which none or few can afford cannot very seriously be called a right at all. Only a slender percentage of Boston's many thousand Negro families could afford to take advantage of "Open Enrollment." The cost for any man of transporting his own child to school every day was far too great. It was also well known to what extent local principals threw obstacles in the way of Negro children who were seeking to obtain transfers to white schools, and it was equally well known what Mrs. Hicks herself thought about such transfers. Despite such facts, however, and despite such acknowledged attitudes, Mrs. Hicks not only made the statement but allowed it to rest as one of the foundations of her case. When she had struck on a phrase or formula that seemed to be appealing to her voters, she had the persistence and doggedness and sheer political intelligence to stick to it, no matter how many times it might have been refuted or disproven.

One of the teachers at my school told me of this incident concerning Mrs. Hicks: At a meeting held a few years ago at the time of a major school stay-out in this area, when Negro leaders led large numbers of Negro parents in keeping their children out

of classes for one day, Mrs. Hicks stood up in front
of a group of maybe 100 assembled teachers and
cried out, with tears streaming from her eyes: "God
forgive them for they know not what they do!" At
this point, according to the story, most of the Negro
teachers present stood up and walked out. From the
position of Mrs. Hicks, if the quotation is correct,
the leaders of the Negro community were taking the
part of anti-Christs and murderers. They were endangering the existence of Mrs. Hicks by demanding
to be treated as Americans. I think this is a good
example of the manner in which she and many
other politicians have been able to turn the tables
on the Negro community. Her posture throughout
has been one of injured benevolence and of misunderstood good will. It has been very effective with
the voters, but it is not the truth.

The Interim Report itemized the following areas
of concern:

There were 45 schools in Boston with over 50
per cent non-white, 28 with over 80 per cent, 16 with
96 percent or above. Among the highest in the city:
the William Lloyd Garrison School, with 96.8 percent non-white. One school (the Hyde) had 99.1.
One: 99.5. One (the Lewis Annex) did not have one
child who was white. If this was not de facto segregation in education, then it was difficult to see what
possible meaning that phrase could ever have again.
Statistics that I saw later pin-pointed the discrepancies between amounts of money allocated to the
white and Negro districts. The statistics came from
a report that had been presented to the students
and faculty of the Harvard Divinity School in a
statement of February 20, 1964: 10 per cent lower
textbook expenditures in the Negro schools of Boston, 19 per cent lower library and reference book
expenditures, 27 per cent lower health expenditures
per pupil. In elementary schools over 90 per cent Negro, eight out of nine major items on the educational

budget were lower than in comparable white schools. In schools with an all-white student body, the average ran up to $350 allocated per pupil per year. In three heavily Negro districts, by comparison, the averages were $240, $235, and $232. In-class expenditures for Boston as a whole averaged $275 per pupil. In the Negro schools: $213. It was apparent from this report that Negro areas also had the highest percentage of provisional teachers, those who were fill-ins, had no tenure, no seniority, no experience, and no obligation to remain. These seem amazing facts in a country which daydreams about exporting its democracy. Looking at these figures openly, it is hard not to wonder whether we did not export our democracy a long time ago and now do not have very much of it left for our own people. It is certain that we do not have a great deal of it to spare for Negro children.

SIX

ELICITING the confession of lies out of children who didn't lie and hadn't lied can easily become one of the most highly developed practices within a segregated school. An assumption of prior guilt is often so overwhelming and so absorbing that even a new teacher with strong affiliations to the Negro community, and sometimes even a teacher who is Negro, will be surprised to discover the extent to which he shares it. It seems at moments to require an almost muscular effort of the imagination to consider the possibility in a particular case that the Negro child might actually *not* have done it, that he might *not* be telling any lie. I remember several incidents of this kind when a pupil whom I knew for certain to be innocent was actually brought around to the point of saying, "Yes I did it" or "Yes I was lying," simply from the force of a white adult's accusation.

There was an example of this in the middle of the winter. One morning the Mathematics Teacher came into the Fourth Grade across the stairs from mine when the regular teacher was not present and when I was taking his class while somebody else was filling in with mine. The children had done an arithmetic assignment the day before. All but two had had it graded and passed back. The two who didn't get it back insisted to me that they had done it but that the substitute teacher who had been with them the day before must have thrown it aside or lost it. I had been in and out of that room long enough to know those two boys and to believe what they were saying. I also knew that in the chaos of substitute changes there was a continual loss and mislaying of homework and of papers of all sorts. Despite this, the Math Teacher came into the room in a mood of anger, delivered a withering denunciation to the whole class on their general performance, then addressed herself to the two boys whose papers had not been given back. She called them to the front and, without questioning or qualifications, she *told* them that they were lying and that she knew they were lying and, furthermore, that she did not want contradictions from them because she knew them too well to be deceived. The truth is that she did not know them at all and probably did not even know their names or who they were. What she meant that she knew was "children who are like them"—in this case, "Negro nine-year-old boys who like to tell lies." Knowing them or not, however, she descended upon them in her manner and she told them that they were liars and did it with so much vigor that she virtually compelled them to believe it must be so. She wasn't the only one in our school who could break down a child by that method, but she was one of the most effective at it.

A somewhat different incident of this sort concerned another boy and involved one of the male teachers in our school. One day while I was working I saw this teacher coming toward me and holding a boy named Anthony rather firmly by the arm. I asked my class to sit still a moment while I went out behind the portable blackboard to find out what was going on. The teacher continued to hold Anthony firmly by the arm. He stood Anthony before me. Anthony looked down at the floor: a common focus at our school for the intimidated eyes of Negro boys. I knew him only slightly. He was one of the slow readers who met with me for extra work from time to time. In this case, I had not seen him for a number of days.

"ANTHONY," said the teacher, "I WANT YOU TO

TELL   MR.   KOZOL   NOW   THE   SAME   THING
THAT   YOU   TOLD   ME."

It was spaced out like that, exactly, with a caesura
of intensity and measured judgment and of per-
suasive intelligence in between every parceled word:
"I   WANT   YOU   TO   GO   ON   NOW   AND
SAY   TO   MR.   KOZOL   WHAT   YOU   WANT   TO
TELL   HIM   AND   I   WANT   YOU   TO   SAY   IT
IN   A   VOICE   WHICH   IS   LOUD   AND   CLEAR
AND   I   WANT   YOU   TO   LOOK   UP   AT   MR.
KOZOL."

When he spoke this way it was as if every child, or
every person, in the whole world might be an isolated
idiot and that, if the words did not come out so slow
and careful, nobody in the world might ever truly
find out what any other person believed. Sometimes
I think that many teachers in these schools make the
mistake of attributing their own obtuseness or sense
of isolation to the children they are teaching and
that, having little faith in the communication of man
to man themselves, they do not really believe you
can get through to children either unless you spell
everything out in these awful singsong terms.

"ANTHONY," the teacher continued, "MR.   KOZOL
IS   A   VERY   BUSY   MAN.   MR.   KOZOL   HAS
A   WHOLE   CLASS   OF   CHILDREN   WAITING.
NOW   WE   DON'T   WANT   TO   KEEP   MR.   KO-
ZOL   STANDING   HERE   AND   WAITING   FOR   YOU,   AN-
THONY,   DO   WE?   AND   WE   WOULDN'T   WANT
MR.   KOZOL   TO   THINK   THAT   WE   WERE
AFRAID   TO   SPEAK   UP   AND   APOLOGIZE   TO
HIM   WHEN   WE   HAVE   DONE   SOMETHING
WRONG.   WOULD   WE   WANT   MR.   KOZOL   TO
THINK   THAT,   ANTHONY?"

Anthony kept his eyes on the floor. My students
poked and peered and stared and craned their necks
around from behind the broken blackboard. At last
I could see that Anthony had decided to give in.
With one of the most cynical yet thoroughly re-
pentant looks of confession that I have ever seen in

any person's eyes, he looked up first at the teacher, then at me, and said decently: "I'm sorry." And the teacher said to him: "I'm sorry—WHO?" And Anthony said nicely: "I'm sorry, Mr. Kozol." And the teacher said: "Good boy, Anthony!" or something of that sort and he touched him in a nice way on the arm. Now the truth is: He *had* been a good boy. He had been a very good boy indeed. He had been a good boy in exactly this regard: that he had gone along with the assumption of one white man about one Negro, had done nothing at all to contradict or to topple that conception, and he even had acted out and executed agreeably a quite skillful little confessional vignette to reinforce it. To this day, I have not the slightest idea of what he had done wrong, or whether he had even done anything at all.

When something as crazy as this happens, I think that it is important to find out how it could be possible. How can an adult so easily, so heedlessly and so unhesitatingly attribute to a child the blame for a misdemeanor about which he has so little information and about which, in fact, he may know nothing? I am sure some of the reasons are the same as those for the frequent use of the rattan: haste and hurry, fear on the part of teachers, animosity and resentment and the potentiality for some sort of sudden insurrection on the parts of certain children. The atmosphere at times becomes so threatening to many teachers that they dare not risk the outbreak of disorder which might occur if they should take time to ascertain gently and carefully and moderately the actual nature of what is really going on. It always seems more practical and less risky to pretend to know more than you do and to insist on your omniscience. When you assume a child is lying and tell him so without reservations, he is almost inclined to agree with you, and furthermore it is often to his advantage to do so since in this way he is likely to minimize his punishment. A child, of course, who begins by pretending to accept blame may end

up by *really* accepting it. If you pretend something
well, and if that pretense becomes a habit, and if
that habit in time becomes the entire style and
strategy with which you deal with the white world,
then probably it is not surprising if at last it gets
into your bloodstream too and begins to feed your
body. Naturally all children don't react in the same
way and, among the children at my school, there
were many different degrees of blame-acceptance or
resignation or docility. There were also children who
did not give in at all. It was not these—not the
defiant ones—but the children who gave in to their
teachers most easily and utterly who seemed the
saddest.

I noticed this one day while I was out in the auditorium doing reading with some children: Classes
were taking place on both sides of us. The Glee Club
and the sewing classes were taking place at the same
time in the middle. Along with the rest, there was a
Fifth Grade remedial math group, comprising six
pupils, and there were several other children whom
I did not know about simply walking back and forth.
Before me were six Fourth Graders, most of them
from the disorderly Fourth Grade and several of
them children who had had substitute teachers during much of the previous two years. It was not their
fault; they had done nothing to deserve substitute
teachers. And it was not their fault now if they could
not hear my words clearly since it also was true that
I could barely hear theirs. Yet the way that they
dealt with this dilemma, at least on the level at
which I could observe it, was to blame, not the
school but themselves. Not one of those children
would say to me: "Mr. Kozol, it's too noisy." Not
one of them would say: "Mr. Kozol, what's going on
here? This is a crazy place to learn."

This instead is what I heard:

"Mr. Kozol, I'm trying as hard as I can but I just
can't even hear a word you say."

"Mr. Kozol, please don't be angry. It's so hard—I couldn't hear you."

"Mr. Kozol—please would you read it to me one more time?"

You could not mistake the absolute assumption that this mess was not only their own fault but something to be ashamed of. It was a triumph of pedagogic brainwashing. The place was ugly, noisy, rotten. Yet the children before me found it natural and automatic to accept as normal the school's structural inadequacies and to incorporate them, as it were, right into themselves: as if perhaps the rotting timbers might be not objective calamities but self-condemning configurations of their own making and as if the frenzied noise and overcrowding were a condition and an indictment not of the school building itself but rather of their own inadequate mentalities or of their own incapacitated souls. Other children were defiant but most of them were not. It was the tension between defiance and docility, and the need of a beleaguered teacher to justify something absolutely unjustifiable, which created the air of unreality, possible danger, intellectual hypocrisy and fear. The result of this atmosphere was that too many children became believers in their own responsibility for being ruined and they themselves, like the teachers, began somehow to believe that some human material is just biologically better and some of it worse. A former chairman and present member of the Boston School Committee, a person named William O'Connor, has publicly given utterance to this idea in words he must regret by this time. "We have no inferior education in our schools," he has let himself be quoted: "What we have been getting is an inferior type of student." Is it any wonder, with the heads of the school system believing this, that after a while some of the children come to believe they are inferior too?

SEVEN

THE attitudes of many teachers, I suppose, are derived over the course of years from the kinds of books they use. Many of the books we had at school were very bad for many reasons, and none of them that I recall was very good. I was promised a certain amount of new material during the year, but this material did not appear. The only new material that I had received by the middle of the winter was an expensive boxed edition of *The Bobbsey Twins*. The old books with which we were already saddled confirmed for me almost all of the criticism that I had ever heard about conventional texts, except that perhaps the ones we had outstripped the criticism a little. Of four biographical series that were available in our Fourth Grade classrooms, out of a total of 140 biographies of famous men and women, there was one that had to do with a Negro. That one was George Washington Carver. The geography book given to my pupils and kept within their desks or on their shelves, was about eighteen years old in substance, though it was somewhat newer than that by renewal of copyright. In this book, typical of many others in its title as it was also in approach and manner, a traditional American cross-country journey was traced. During this journey there wasn't one mention, hint, whisper or glimmer of a dark-skinned face. Reading it without any outside source of information, you would have had no reason to suspect either the past history or present existence of a Negro race. The chapter on the South described an idyllic and fantasied landscape in the heart of Dixie: pastoral home of hard-working white citizens, contented white children and untroubled white adults. Cotton production was studied, and a vicarious journey to a Mississippi plantation was undertaken, without ever a reference to, or picture of, a dark-skinned person.

The history book could not get by in the same manner. It had to speak of Negroes because it had to speak of slavery. It did this, however, in a manner that seemed reluctant and half-hearted. "Men treasure freedom above all else," the narrative told us at one point. But it balanced this out by telling us beforehand that "most Southern people treated their slaves kindly. 'Our slaves have good homes and plenty to eat. When they are sick, we take care of them . . .'" In the final event I think that the author came out on the side of emancipation, but he did this in a tone and style which were so lukewarm and insipid as to be without effect. The language used throughout was coy and awkward: "In the dictionary we find that one meaning of the word 'civil' is 'polite.' The Civil War was not a polite one. It was a war between the states of Our America . . ." A final verdict on the War Between the States was the following: "No one can truly say, 'The North was right' or 'The Southern cause was the better.' Remember, each side fought for the ideals it believed in. For in Our America all of us have the right to our beliefs."

The material about the Civil War was not the only disturbing section in this book, but it is the part that seems most relevant. It would always have been simple enough, if I had been obliged to use that section, just to skip over the offensive pages—or, better, not to skip them but rather to read them with the children and then to deal with them critically. Since that time, I have done this in many situations and I do it frequently today. Nonetheless, the fact remained: The book had been printed. The book had been stocked and ordered. The book stood within our bookshelves and it was looked into by dozens of children every day. I wondered for how many years it would continue to misrepresent reality in this manner and to how many future thousands of Negro children it would spread the sad word that their people in bondage did not have the imagination to be free?

There is a school in Boston named for William Lloyd Garrison. It was at this school that the class to which I have referred received twenty-five substitute teachers in the fall of 1964. I once had a chance to work for a few mornings with a group of Fourth, Fifth and Sixth Grade pupils from the Garrison School. I asked them if they would tell me, child by child, the most important facts about the man for whom their school was named. A long silence met my question and then I discovered, by asking some other questions, that not one of these children had the slightest idea either of who he was or of what he had done. No principal, no teacher, it appeared, had ever told them. Some of them had been in that school for six or seven years. They had all studied geography. They had all studied history. They had all, I suppose, talked of current events. Their teachers presumably also had some idea of what was going on in the world and could find the affiliation between this, the present day, and the beliefs of the man whose name had been given to their school. The school happened to be one of the most totally segregated (96.8 per cent) in all of Boston. Yet none of these children knew who William Lloyd Garrison was. So long as a school that is 96.8 per cent Negro can stand in the name of William Lloyd Garrison and so long as teachers and principals are unable to tell the children in whose name their building stands, then I don't think it will be surprising that geography and history books will also resort to evasions about America and it will not be surprising either that Negro children, growing a little older, will look back with cynicism and surely without forgiveness upon the white teachers who have denied them even this much self-knowledge and who have disseminated among them these crippling ideas and desiccating lies.

When we got to the cotton chapter in the geography book I have described, I decided to alter somewhat the program that the Reading Teacher scheduled. Since I couldn't throw out the textbook and was required to make use of it, and since its use, despite anything I could say, was going to create a certain kind of harm and leave behind a certain kind of poison, I got the idea of supplying the class with extra material in the form of a mimeographed sheet that would afford them the benefit of the truth in at least one area. I did not have any intention of telling the children about lynchings, beatings, murders. I did not propose to tell them any tales about the Ku Klux Klan. All I thought I would like to do was to add to the study of cotton-growing a little parcel of information about the connection between the discovery of Eli Whitney's cotton gin and the greater growth of slavery. I wrote these words:

"Eli Whitney invented the cotton gin in 1793 . . . The cotton gin was a machine for separating the cotton from the cotton seeds. Until it was invented, this process took many people hundreds of hours of work. Now it could be done quickly . . . More people began growing cotton and their plantations became bigger and bigger. As a result of this, more and more farmworkers were needed to plant and pick the cotton. This was why so many Negro slaves were brought from Africa. The white people did not feel like doing the hard work for themselves . . . It is easy to see that the cotton gin made cotton important to the South, and also that it is cotton that made it useful to have slaves."

I had to submit this to the Reading Teacher, and

I would like to describe her reaction in detail because it represents so effectively the attitude of a great many of the other teachers in my school. Before doing this, I should explain that this took place during a time of great turbulence in the South and that teachers and children alike were seeing in the papers and watching on television the news stories about the murders of white and Negro people in Mississippi and about the many other forms of lawlessness and racism which were becoming so common in certain sections of the country. It also was the winter which was to culminate tragically, during March, in the clubbing and subsequent death in Selma, Alabama of James Reeb, a young white minister from our neighborhood of Roxbury. Certain of the realities of life in America and in the South, therefore, were very much in all our minds, and they clashed grotesquely, in my thinking, with the sound of the material that I was being asked to teach in school.

I think that many other teachers worked hard to shut out these shocking realities from the school building and that some were able to do it quite successfully. I have the impression, for example, that the Reading Teacher had done this to the degree where she was able to spend almost her entire day in school in something like a cloud of benevolence and golden feeling, and without ever the slightest idea or dream of what might be going on outside. In a grim way, I liked better the response of a redneck teacher who simply came out and said bluntly one day that it was the minister's own damn fault for getting killed, because if he didn't go down there and try to stir up the niggers in the first place, the whole thing never would have happened. I don't think that it is quite so vicious or malignant or even dangerous to pupils to come straight out and admit that you can't stand them as it is to go on and on in the way that the Reading Teacher did, and to pretend endlessly that you have some kind of massive and inscrutable and all-enveloping love for the very children whom you are at that moment destroying. It is one of the interesting and odd things about that year that, looking back, I feel so much more involvement with, and even hopefulness about, that outright bigot who called the Southern Negroes niggers than I do about the pious maiden ladies who will probably go on forever thinking that they love the people they are killing. It also seems notable that that redneck rough guy who could at times be so physically vicious to the kids at least was not the slightest bit scared to speak up about race issues and about Negro problems in his class, while so many of the other teachers, and the Reading Teacher in particular, seemed scared to death even to spit out a word like "Negro" for fear that somebody might think they were prejudiced.

The day that James Reeb died in Selma, Alabama, I remember that the Reading Teacher caught me out in the hallway and took my arm in an affectionate and possessive manner. Obviously taken with much emotion, she spoke with what I took for genuine horror of the recent events in Alabama and of the dreadful things that were being done to people there. But then she looked up at me and added, with an inexplicable resurgence of bouncy optimism and of scarcely believable satisfaction:

"Thank God at least, Johnny, that we can come to school each morning and do our work and forget about things like Alabama while we are here!"

I said this to her: "I am sorry that I don't feel that way. To me, Alabama is this school."

She seemed startled, and offended.

Perhaps, then, it is not surprising that she reacted as she did to my proposed material on slavery and cotton. I recall clearly the moment after I had handed her that sheet of paper and as I stood before her, waiting, beside the doorway that led out into

the large hall. Looking over the paper, she agreed
with me immediately that it was accurate. Nobody,
she said, was going to quibble with the idea that
cotton and the cotton gin and slavery were all pretty
much intertwined. But it was the question of the
"advisability of any mention of slavery to the children at this time" which, she said, she was presently
turning over in her mind. Would it, she asked me
frankly, "truly serve the advantage of the children
at this stage to confuse and complicate the study of
simple geography with socio-economic facts?" Was it
relevant, she was asking essentially, to the understanding of the production of cotton to hook on any
riders about slaves? She then said something which
must have seemed absolutely innocent to her while
she was saying it but which I should think, looking
back upon it later, she must have found awkward
and uncomfortable to recall. She said, with the very
opposite of malice but only with an expression of
the most intense and honest affection for the children in the class:

"I don't want these children to have to think back
on this year later on and to have to remember that
we were the ones who told them they were Negro."

The amount of difficulty involved in telling children they are Negro, of course, is proportional to
the degree of ugliness which is attached to that word
within a person's mind. I believe that, in the Reading Teacher's mind, the word lived in company with
a great deal of ugliness. The fact that she could have
spoken in this manner, however, and done it so innocently and so baldly, seems to me an extraordinary commentary both on our nation in general and
on the nature of the Boston schools. What she was
afraid of was to be remembered as the one who told
them that they were what they *are*. But this is exactly what I was trying to tell them every single
day on almost every little pretext that I had. Why
would a teacher fear it? Would it be a thing of which

to be afraid? Would it be to tell them something shameful? Would it be equivalent to telling them that they were bad—or hateful? They were Negro. To be taught by a teacher who felt that it would be wrong to let them know it must have left a silent and deeply working scar. The extension to children of the fears and evasions of a teacher is probably not very uncommon, and at times the harm it does is probably trivial. But when it comes to a matter of denying to a class of children the color of their skin and of the very word that designates them, then I think that it takes on the proportions of a madness.

In time, at school, we finished our journey across America. Next we were to go for an imaginary trip across the sea. We were to study about the Arabs and, before we had really begun, the Reading Teacher came in once again and urged upon me a book which she said that she had used with the children in her own classes for a great many years. From this book she asked me to pick out a good section to read. It was not the same geography book that the children had at their desks. She told me that she considered it a better one, but that it was too old to be in regular use. We were studying the desert. The night before, I looked into the book, and I found some remarkable writing. It is fortunate that I looked carefully and made myself some warning marks before I just walked into the class and started to read. These are some of the things I found as I looked through this book:

"The streets of this Oasis city of Biskra are interesting. There are many different people upon them. Some who are white like ourselves have come here from Europe. Others are Negroes with black skins, from other parts of Africa. And many are bronze-faced Arabs who have come in from the desert to trade in the stores . . ."

There next is a description of an Arab family: "We meet Ali and Selma and their family near the market place. The Bedouin father is tall and straight. He wears a robe that falls to his ankles, and his bare feet are shod in sandals of camel's leather . . . Behind the Bedouin father walk his wife and his children, Ali and Selma. The Bedouin mother is dressed in a long robe. She, too, wears a cloth over her head to protect it from the sun. Ali and Selma wear clothing like that of their father and mother. Their brown feet are bare and covered with dust.

"These people are fine looking. Their black eyes are bright and intelligent. Their features are much like our own, and although their skin is brown, they belong to the white race, as we do. It is the scorching desert sun that has tanned the skin of the Arabs to such a dark brown color."

After I read this, I was curious to see how the authors would treat the African Negroes. I looked ahead until I found these words:

"The black people who live on this great continent of Africa were afraid of the first white men who came to explore their land. They ran and hid from them in the dark jungle. They shot poisoned arrows from behind the thick bushes. They were savage and un-civilized."

The more I read, the more I thought I could understand why those African people may well have had good reason to be afraid of the first white men: "Yumbu and Minko are a black boy and a black girl who live in this jungle village. Their skins are of so dark a brown color that they look almost black. Their noses are large and flat. Their lips are thick. Their eyes are black and shining, and their hair is so curly that it seems like wool. THEY ARE NEGROES AND THEY BELONG TO THE BLACK RACE."

Turning the pages to a section about Europe, I read by contrast the following description of a very different, and presumably more attractive, kind of child: "Two Swiss children live in a farmhouse on the edge of town . . . These children are handsome.

Their eyes are blue. Their hair is golden yellow. Their white skins are clear, and their cheeks are as red as ripe, red apples."

What I felt about the words that I have capitalized above was not that they were wrong, or that there could conceivably ever be anything wrong about saying of a group of people that they are members of a particular race, but simply that the context and the near-belligerence of the assertion make it *sound* degrading. It is not in the facts. It is only in the style. I capitalized those lines, but they feel capitalized when you read them. They are arbitrary in their finality and the feeling they convey is one of categorical and, somehow, almost syntactical ill-fate. It is from reading a book like this over the course of twenty years that the Reading Teacher and thousands of other teachers like her might well come to believe that you would do a child nothing but a disservice to let him know that he was Negro. The books are not issued any more—but the teachers still are. It seems to me that until something has been done to affect those teachers, and to alter the attitudes with which they approach the children in their charge, then none of the other changes are going to make a very great difference, and the overall atmosphere is likely to remain the same.

Accompanying the text about the Congo in this book there were some gory illustrations: half-naked Africans in what are sometimes called characteristic poses, beating on drums and puckering out their mouths and looking truly strange. There was a photograph of the Pygmies which seemed to make fun of them and, if it is possible, to "shrink" them and make them look even littler than they really are. A straight and handsome tall white hunter is seen surrounded by tiny, swarming naked people. Their bellies look bloated and a number of them are gripping arrows or spears. We read these words:

"The most interesting of all the tribes we see upon

the Congo are the tiny Pygmies. The full-grown men and women of the Pygmy tribes do not weigh more than a seven-year-old American child. Their children look like little brown dolls. These Pygmies are Negroes."

There are few uses in this chapter of such words as "skillful," "well-developed," "pride," "decency," "fine-looking," "dignity" or any of the other galaxies of affirmative nouns and modifiers which are reserved in these kinds of books for those of Anglo-Saxon stock or those who are sufficiently close to Anglo-Saxons to share a part of their white pride. At the end of this section, the author suggests that it is the presence of the white man within Africa which allows some room for hope:

"Our airplane circles over the grasslands and then flies back again down the Congo to the capital city of Leopoldville. This town has many white people living in it." The point of this, the intention, seems to be that the reader will feel relieved. "Most are from Belgium, the country of Europe that has made the Congo Valley its colony. The Belgians govern the Congo. They run the steamships and the railroads. They have set out plantations of cotton, sugar cane, peanuts, and cacao, and they direct the work of gathering rubber from the wild Hevea trees . . . They mine the copper in the mining districts and they direct the trading stations . . . They believe that they can develop the country better than the chiefs of the savage tribes, who know so little about modern ways."

In the same book there was also some strange writing about the Chinese. In this case it was not that we were told anything was wrong with looking odd or peculiar but simply that we were made to feel, beyond possibilities of redemption, that this "oddness," this "differentness," this "peculiarity" is something from which we can feel ourselves indescribably lucky to have been spared. It is the inexorable quality of differentness which seems so evil here. A bitter little perjury is perpetrated upon children even before they are old enough to understand exactly why it is that the things that are made to seem so different, strange and peculiar, are precisely the things which it is easiest to despise. Of Chinese children: "They are different in appearance from any other children we have seen. Their skins are creamy yellow and their black eyes are set under narrow slanting lids. Their hair is black and coarse, and their cheek bones are high. They belong to the yellow race."

Looking at material like this, Americans may be forced to wonder what kind of country we were thirty years ago when this book was published. But then we also are forced to wonder whether we are really entirely changed today. For the alterations in many of the textbooks have not been enormous, and even in those where the apparent change has been considerable, the deeper change is slight. It may seem discouraging to add this but some of the worst among the newer books are worst precisely for the reason that they are trying so self-consciously and so pathetically to erase or to compensate for the prejudices of the earlier books. One of this kind, for example, used by one of the other Fourth Grade teachers at my school, was called *Journeys Through Many Lands*. In this book, as in the one discussed above, there was again no mention of any American Negroes but the authors at least made an heroic effort to overcome their repugnance to the African blacks. This, however, is what happens when people of good intention attempt to overcome a conditioned repugnance and to summon up complimentary words:

After they had given the Pygmies the same sort of drubbing that they get elsewhere, the authors of this book went on to admire the taller and, to them, more attractive Grassland Negroes. "These Negroes," said the authors, "are stronger and more intelligent than the Pygmies. They are fine, big black fellows . . ." After that, the authors went on to say that these "fine, big black fellows" had plenty of admirable qualities and for those qualities they were then given unstinting praise. But the language that had been used seemed to ruin everything afterward. You could picture the British or American ambassador from a hundred years ago watching the Negroes filing before him in the jungle and offering that kind of cruel, misguided praise. But this is the question, disquieting or not, to which an answer must be given: How long can the parents of any Negro child in a nation which talks about democracy and fair play be expected to stand by in passivity and patience while their child sweats out his lessons and drains away his self-respect and dignity in the obedient study of such books as these? It does not even matter if all of these books should be found out, discovered, filtered off and taken away. The teachers who believe in those books are still teaching and until they stop teaching, or stop believing, the assumptions will live on and the dignity of the children will decay.

EIGHT

ALL books used in a school system, merely by the law of averages, are not going to be blatantly and consistently bad. A larger number of the books we had in Boston were either quietly and subtly bad, or else just devastatingly bad only in one part. One such book, not used in my school but at the discipline school, was entitled *Our World Today*. It seems useful to speak about it here because it exemplifies to perfection the book which might be remarkably accurate or even inspired in its good intentions in one section and then brutally clumsy, wrong and stupid in another. Right and wrong, good and bad, alternate in this book from sentence to sentence and from page to page:

"The people of the British Isles are, like our own, a mixed people. Their ancestors were the sturdy races of northern Europe, such as Celts, Angles, Saxons, Danes, and Normans, whose energy and abilities still appear in their descendants. With such a splendid inheritance what could be more natural than that the British should explore and settle many parts of the world, and, in time, build up the world's greatest colonial empire?"

"The people of South Africa have one of the most democratic governments now in existence in any country."

"Africa needs more capitalists . . . White managers are needed . . . to show the Negroes how to work and to manage the plantations . . ."

"In our study of the nations of the world, we

should try to understand the people and their problems from their point of view. We ought to have a sympathetic attitude toward them, rather than condemn them through ignorance because they do not happen always to have our ways."

"The Negro is very quick to imitate and follow the white man's way of living . . ."

". . . The white man may remain for short periods and direct the work, but he cannot . . . do the work himself. He must depend upon the natives to do the work."

"The white men who have entered Africa are teaching the natives how to live."

Something similar to this, though it was not in a printed textbook, was a mimeographed test about American history that the Fourth Grade teachers at my school had been using for several years. The test listed a number of attributes and qualities that were supposed to have been associated with George Washington: "courageous, rich, intelligent, wise, handsome, kind, good in sports, patient, believed in God, sense of humor, dressed in style, rode a horse well." From these the class were asked to underline the things that made George Washington "a great leader." The answers that would get points were only the noble virtues. "Rich," "handsome," "dressed in style," "rode a horse well" and "good in sports" were wrong. It was, I felt, not really a lesson on George Washington but a force-feeding of a particular kind of morality:

THESE ARE GOOD QUALITIES.

GEORGE WASHINGTON GOT SOMEPLACE.

THESE MUST BE THE THINGS THAT MADE HIM GREAT.

What had happened, very clearly, was that the right answers had never been derived from a real study of George Washington but rather they were taken from somebody's cupboard of good qualities ("moral builders") and then *applied* to George Washington exactly like plaster or paint. All the things listed were assumed to be true of him, but only the moral uplifters could be considered to be the things that helped him to be great. I thought this wrong for several reasons. One reason simply was a matter of accuracy: George Washington was not really a very handsome man so it seemed unwise and dumbly chauvinistic to say he was. Another mistake, though it is a small one, was that he did not really have much of a sense of humor and people have even said that he was rather short-tempered. On the subject of his religion, it seemed presumptuous to me, and rather risky, to make any statements at all in regard to a belief in God about which, if it was really so, only George Washington himself could have known. On the opposite side, we do know well that good looks and lots of money have helped many men and do not even necessarily diminish them but have formed romantic parts of their greatness. This was true, for example, of President Kennedy, and it does him no dishonor to say so. What does do a man dishonor is to paint him up in false colors which we either do not know about or which we do know about and know that he did not have. I spoke to the Reading Teacher about this and I pointed out to her that it seemed to me Washington's wealth would not be at all a bad answer. The matter of his belief in God seemed questionable. The Reading Teacher did not often get openly angry with me, but she did on this occasion.

"That's out of the question! We are not going to start teaching cynicism here in the Fourth Grade."

I found myself equally angry. I said that I did not think that it would be teaching cynicism at all, but quite the reverse. I said I thought children should learn now, and the sooner the better, that money frequently, and more often than not, counted for more than religious intensity in the political world. I also said that I thought it was a far greater kind of cynicism to dish out to them at this age a fatuous and lyrical idealism which was going to get smashed down to the ground the first time that any one of them went out into the City of Boston and just tried to get himself a decent job, let alone try to follow George Washington on the strength of such qualities as "patience," "sense of humor," "belief in God," and hope to become President of the United States with the kind of education they were getting here. I said I thought that the highest cynicism of all was not to let the people in a running-race have any knowledge of the odds. I said that the only way in which one of these children ever *could* be President was if he understood absolutely and as soon as possible how many fewer advantages he had than had been the fortune of George Washington. With that knowledge first, not cynical in the least but having a true connection with the world, then those admired qualities might perhaps be the attributes of greatness, but not without a prior sense of the real odds.

When I began to talk about some of these things more openly, as I did now more frequently with the Reading Teacher, she would tell me sometimes that, temperamentally, she agreed with my ideas and did not believe that in themselves they were wrong but that to teach such things to the children "at this level and at this stage" was something that she could not allow because this was "not the proper age at which to start to break things down." The Fourth Grade, she told me in some real awkwardness and verbal confusion (which made me feel guilty for having brought the subject up), was the age "in which a teacher ought to be building up things and ideas." Later on, she seemed to be saying, there would be time to knock the same things down. I thought this a little like a theory of urban renewal, but it seemed a kind of renewal program that was going to cost somebody dearly. It was to erect first the old rotten building (pollyanna voyages, a nation without

Negroes, suburban fairy tales, pictures in pastel shades), let it all stand a year or two until it began to sway and totter, then tear it down and, if the wreckage could be blasted, put up a new, more honest building in its spot. If a city planner ever came up with a theory like that, I should think he would be laughed out of business. Yet this was not very different from the Reading Teacher's view of children and of education. There was a lot in the Boston curriculum, furthermore, to support her.

I've said something about the social studies books and teacher attitudes already. One thing I've scarcely mentioned is the curriculum material in literature and reading. Probably this would be the best place to make some reference to it, for nothing could better typify the image of the crumbling school structure than the dry and deadly basic reading textbooks that were in use within my school. Most of these books were published by Scott, Foresman. The volume aimed at Third Graders, used for slow Fourth Graders at my school, was called *New Streets and Roads*. No title could have been farther from the mark. Every cliché of bad American children's literature seemed to have been contained within this book. The names of the characters describe the flavor of the stories: Betty Jane Burns and Sarah Best and Miss Molly and Fluffy Tail and Miss Valentine of Maple Grove School . . . The children in my class had been hearing already for several years about Birmingham and Selma and tear-gas and cattle-prods and night-courts and slum-lords—and jazz. To expect these children to care about books which even very comfortable suburban children would probably have found irrelevant and boring seemed to me futile. Yet there were no other books around. These were the only ones we had. I wondered if it was thought that the proper way to teach reading to slow Fourth Graders was by foisting upon them a pablum out of nursery land. Possibly it was a benevolent school-lady's most dearly held belief that she could shut out the actual world in this manner and could make the world of these growing Negro children as neat and aseptic as her own. It may have been another belief that a few dozen similarly inclined white ladies in a few dozen Negro classrooms with a few hundred pure white texts would be able to overcome taste and appetite, sight and sound. I didn't think so. The books seemed so overwhelmingly boring. Wouldn't the children find them boring too? The look of boredom seemed always so apparent in the faces of those children. The books did not refer to them. What did refer to them was obvious.

Once I asked a class to think of a sentence using both the word "glass" and the word "house." The first answer I received told me that "there is a lot of glass out back of my house."

To a boy in the reading group: "Do you know an antonym for dry?"

"Mr. Kozol—isn't there something called a dry martini?"

The Reading Teacher's reactions to these kinds of student responses, when I related them to her, were generally pretty much the same:

"We cannot use books that are sordid."

"Children do not like gloomy stories."

"I haven't seen any evidence that children like to read especially about things that are real."

I suppose it is true that the children she took out for reading generally were attentive, at least on a temporary basis, to the texts that she was using with them, but I think there were two special reasons for this. One reason was that she could "sell" almost anything to anyone if she wanted, being such a very experienced and such an intensely persuading teacher. The other was that the children, in reading with docility and in writing without their own imagination, were always more than willing to confirm a

white teacher's idea of them and to put forward
in their writings and conversations not what they
really felt or dreamed but what they had good reason by now to know that she wanted to believe about
them. I was not asking for children's books to be
sordid, either, but the Reading Teacher was pretty
much suggesting an identity between *sordid* and
real. I had the idea that to build upon some of
the things the children already knew would be more
fruitful than to deny them. I also had a suspicious,
ungenerous feeling about the reluctance of the white
teachers to make use of more realistic books. Their
argument, stated one way or another, was that such
books might be bad for the children but I thought
that that was not what they really believed. I thought
the denial came not from a fear that such things might
be bad for the child but rather from a certainty
that they would be bad for the teacher. I thought
that the Reading Teacher and the Deputy Superintendent and many others like them would have been
confused to be told that the world of those Negro
children was in a great many cases a good deal more
interesting and more vital than their own. It seemed
to me that what they were trying ineffectively to do
was to replace a very substantial and by no means
barren lower-class culture with a concoction of pretty
shopworn middle-class ideas. The ideas they intro-
duced, moreover, did not even have the joy of being
exuberant, for they were mainly the values of a
parched and parochial and rather grim and beaten
lower middle-class and were, I felt, inferior by many
times to that which the children and their parents
already had. More succinctly, what I mean is that
the real trouble with perpetrating such colorless
materials upon very colorful children was not only
that the weak culture they purveyed was out of
kilter with the one the children already had, but
that it also was mediocre by comparison.

There was another problem in the basic readers.

This was the old and obvious one of inherited tales of time-worn prejudice:

"Once upon a time there was a woman who had two daughters. One of them was beautiful, but the other one was ugly."

When you read this, you may look up at the illustration on the top of the page but you know, even before you look, which daughter is going to have yellow hair and which one will have dark hair. The dark-skinned girl, the bad one, also has pimples or some kind of coal-smudge beneath her nose, along her cheek and on her jaw. In the story each of these daughters goes for a visit under the ground to stay with a mysterious lady. Each behaves according to her kind. The good daughter behaves nicely, works hard, and receives as her reward a rain of gold coins. The other daughter behaves poorly, refuses to do any work, is selfish, wants something for nothing, and receives as her punishment a shower of black tar. "The tar did not come off the girl until she stopped being lazy," the author tells us. "And it was a long time before she learned that lesson."

In such a way as this, a point perhaps dear to generations of white school-ladies and moralistic educators is gotten across, but it must be obvious that such a point as this no longer can be either dear or acceptable to Negro people. Yet nothing or next to nothing had been done at the time of my teaching to get rid of these kinds of books. Again, as with the social studies books, when the editor of one of these readers went out of his way to find something that would have to do with Negroes, it tended to be embarrassing and awkward. One instance of this was a story called "You Never Can Tell." The story seems memorable because, so far as I can recall, it is the only story in any storybook on any shelf that I ever saw within my school in which an American Negro child was described. The problem about the story was that it could not present the child in anything but a slavelike, superstitious and pathetic-comic light. The Negroes were described not with malice but with condescension as the funny, sad and sweet little wandering attendants to a supercilious, incredibly distant but also unexpectedly generous white lord.

"Mister Colonel, [said one of the little boys] your horse is mighty dusty from rolling. Peas and I will be proud to brush him up for you."

"Very well," said the Colonel.

The boys borrowed brushes from Big Hand and they brushed the Colonel's horse until he shone like satin in the sunshine.

"I could use two boys like you," the Colonel said, "come to my barn tomorrow and I'll put you to work."

Beans turned to Peas. "Man! We got a job," he said, and he grinned at Peas.

It was not an evil story. If there were others of a different nature also, I know that this one would not have stood out as especially bad. It was only when this stood as the sole literary treatment of an American Negro that it led to the unattractive assumption that the Negro it described was characteristic. In the same way, it was not always a poor African chapter which would be so disturbing in the geography textbook as it was the fact that no counterbalance of any kind existed in an honest treatment of the Negro as an American living in the same land in which the Negro children who were reading the book also lived. There are of course plenty of books that show these things and many of them have been available now for some time and were available at the time that I was teaching. The tutorial programs in Boston were using them and so were many of the more enlightened private schools. I had myself had access to some of these books when I was working as a tutor during the summer before I had come into the schools. The striking thing—the thing that was really revealing and unmistakable—was the force and the lightning-like rate of the resistance that cropped up as soon as I made the first mild offer to bring in a few of these new books to try with my Fourth Grade.

One of these was a book called *Mary Jane*. It had been given to me by one of my summer reading pupils, and told a story about the first Negro girl in a Southern town to attend an all-white school. The child who gave it to me was not a particularly good reader. Yet she had read this book with much involvement and she told me that it made her cry every time she read it again. Another child in the class, no better reader than the first, borrowed the book and read it through in a couple of days. It was 218 pages long. Remembering this now, and confronted every day in school by the monotony and tedium of textbooks, I dug up a few copies of *Mary Jane* and brought them to class with me. They were gone from my table the next day. I got hold of a half-dozen more and they also immediately began to be read. Finally, I ordered from New York about two dozen extra copies so that there were now enough of them for almost every child in my room. I felt the excitement and anticipation that a teacher knows when he recognizes that something unexpected and self-generating is beginning to develop in the classroom. Then it all came to a halt.

The Reading Teacher had gotten wind that the book was in the building and she came up into my room and put her foot down. Her excuse, I remember, was, first, that it would be an excellent book for enrichment for "the very brightest children"—a very few—but that it was infinitely too difficult, too advanced and too sophisticated for use as a regular book. Now it happened to be a fact that one of the slowest readers in my class not only asked me to *sell* her one of my copies but then took it home and read it every night in bed before going to sleep for an entire week until she was finished. She said, when I asked her, that it was the first book she had ever owned in her life. The same sort of thing happened when I brought in half a dozen copies of a children's biography of Martin Luther King. Not only did several children read it with excitement but, when Christmas came, a number of their mothers asked if they could obtain copies from me to give as Christmas gifts. If this curiosity and motivation were so real (and I couldn't think what better proof was needed), then I did not see why we could not allow the larger number of children in the class to read these books too. They were not particularly radical in tone or content. They were not hot-headed and fiery. They were just timely and richly textured books. The Reading Teacher's answer, as I have shown, was first that they were too difficult for most of the pupils (this was not the truth), and then, only latterly, that they were about people who were Negro.

"I wouldn't mind using them," was the way she finally said it to me, "if these were all Negro children in your room. But it would not be fair to the white children in the class to force such books on them too. We do not have all Negroes. If we did, it would be different. I could see using them if this were a segregated school. But it isn't. We have white children. As matters stand it simply would not be right or fair." Whether it was right or fair to the large majority of Negroes to use all white books for their regular work was a question which this otherwise observant lady teacher was not willing to ask. Only whether it would be fair to white children, for once in their lives, to encounter the reverse.

"Things are changing," the Reading Teacher sometimes would say to me as epilogue to these conversations. "I am changing too," she would say. "But everything cannot happen just like that." Yet she had been teaching these children in Roxbury already for a good many years and nothing very much had happened up to now. The schedule for correction of grievances was plotted so slowly. Is there any reason to think it will be different in the future? Next year some integrated readers in a few schools, maybe. And then, with luck, some day later on, they may even use the same kind of racially honest readers in public schools all over town. And some day in those books perhaps it will be a matter not of photographic integration only but of honest inward content too. And then one day possibly not merely the texts but the real children in the real schools also will be integrated and will no longer go to school separately but will be sitting within the same classrooms side by side. In that day, five years, twenty years hence, possibly the teachers as well will begin to think of things differently and will no longer assume that Negro children are poor material because they will not read books that deny them and because they will not work out of their hearts for white teachers who despise them. Perhaps, by the time another generation comes around, the great majority of these things will be corrected. But if I were the parent of a Negro child in school today I know that I would not be able to accept a calendar of improvements that was scaled so slow.

If poison were not spreading at this moment I might agree with the people who say that Negroes ought to sit and wait a little and let some of these things change at their own pace. But when time is destroying the present lives of your own children I do not believe that anyone should wait. No child in the ruined Fourth Grade at my school can ever have that terrible year returned to him. No boy once whipped for society's, not his, wrong is ever again likely to have his whole sense of dignity returned. No young man made to lie and apologize for something he did not do in order to avoid a greater punishment can ever be graced again with the gift of belief in a world or society in which authorities are just. And who in the slow calendar of days in which "things are changing" will find a way, after that change, to give back to the boys at that discipline school the lives that have been taken from them by the Boston Public Schools?

So when a serious woman like the Reading Teacher said to me that things were changing, I thought that it was taking much too long and that things had been changing for one hundred years yet there was still slavery of the deepest kind within these rooms. The slowness of change is always respectable and reasonable in the eyes of the ones who are only watching; it is a different matter for the ones who are in pain. The anger of the Negro mother whose child's years in elementary school have been wasted may seem inexplicable to a person like the Reading Teacher. To me, to that mother, perhaps to some readers also, it is the complacence and the gradualism and the hypocrisy of a woman like the Reading Teacher that seem unjust and strange. It is the comfortable people, by and large—those like the Reading Teacher—who make the decisions in our society. It is only the people that those decisions are going to affect who are expected to stand quietly, and watch patiently, and wait.

NINE

THERE have been some examples in this book already of the degree to which the Boston administrators have been casual, if they have not actually been incompetent, in fulfilling their responsibility to look after even the bare safety of many of the Negro children. The falling-in of a frame of windows on a class of Fourth Grade pupils was one graphic and measurable danger. Another, of which I will speak more a little later, was the school's willingness to hold two crowded classes—one all boys, one all girls— in a dark and dusty and urine-smelling cellar. A more obvious danger, and one for which there seems to be less excuse than for any of the others, was the failure of the school to obtain police cooperation in securing a traffic officer to assist the children in crossing the major avenue that was only a block down from the school. In almost any other urban school system I have heard of, such minimal police protection for five- and six- and seven-year-old children has been a standard practice and expectation. In the case of our own ghetto neighborhood, it seemed that it could by no pressure be achieved. The Principal insisted that she'd requested a lady policeman and that the people up at school headquarters had even appealed to the police directly. Yet nothing was done and one could not help feeling that, in this, as in the area of substitute teachers, unplaced special students and so many of the other characteristic flaws of a segregated school, all the real or pretended efforts of any individual on any one occasion (the

Principal, for example, in saying that in this one case she honestly had tried) just could not be meaningful or truly effective against the greater and overall ineffectiveness and apathy of a white community which simply did not really care and a white community in which, it ought to be remembered, this Principal, like so many other voters and so many teachers, was playing an entirely acquiescent part.

Every effort that she made to replace one broken glass-pane or to let in one new gust of air through one unnailed window was like the effort of a medieval monastic to add one more ecliptic or curve or other trivial alteration to a Ptolemaic system in which he no longer honestly could believe and which everybody could see no longer really worked. She was struggling to save a patchwork system of segregated education by piecemeal projects. But all the small alterations in the world cannot save a system which is rotten. The Principal used to say that she wished, before parents complained about school problems, they would come up first and tell her their worries so that she could get on the phone herself and see what she could get done for them. But this was the offering of a good public relations woman, more than of a humanitarian. For she knew as well as anybody else that the evils inherent in this school that she governed, merely the physical ones, were so rife and so self-multiplying that even if she devoted her whole energies to this one task alone, it still could never get done. Too much was wrong and too deep were the wrongs and too much a part of the wrong was she herself. This is the real answer to her repeated question: "Why don't they just come up and tell me?" And to me she had said, as to the other teachers: "Tell me first when you have any small or large complaints and try not to broadcast it around. Don't forget we are all in a show-window this year."

I disregarded that advice because she had eyes as

well as I and she could see the pasteboard over the
windows as well as I. And she could see welts on
hands, and Second Grade reading scores for Fourth
Grade pupils, and five classes in an auditorium, and
two classes in a basement, and fear in the eyes of
students, and pain in the eyes of mothers, as well
as I. So I did not accept as either honest or serious
her request for frankness, but I viewed it as a political gesture, which in fact is all it was, and I did
not begin to bring her my complaints.

There were four blackboards cutting off my classroom from the auditorium. Two were broken. Yet
these four were all we had to cut us off from the
rest of the hall. One day I saw that one was wob-
bling badly—tottering—and it looked to me as if it
could very easily tip over. Two days went by. On
the third day, the Reading Teacher was getting ready
to do a demonstration English lesson and she began
to turn the blackboard, pushing it from one side with
one hand. The entire unit tipped forward suddenly,
then crashed downward toward the children sitting
two yards off.

It slammed down with a violent impact upon a desk
in the first row. A little girl named Charlene was
sitting in that desk at that moment and she was not
looking up because she had been busy at her work.
The child at that desk missed getting her skull
smashed in by about two and a half inches. The
blackboard remained resting on her desk for a couple
of seconds. The children seemed terrified by the
noise and by the visible proof of how close it had
come. You could see the little girl's head and you
could see the blackboard's edge. There it was. No
doubt. No blur. There was the object. There, a few
inches away, the vulnerable head. I looked. The
Reading Teacher looked. Then there was a kind of
"click" of cancellation and denial and this is what
occurred:

It was as if the film were run backward, as if the

blackboard were lifted up by magic and straightened up nicely and put back to stand where it had been before. The point of it is that the anger and outrage inherent and, one would have thought, inevitable in what had just happened were instantaneously bypassed and ignored. I realized, almost as it happened, how essential and automatic a process this had become within our school. It *had* to be ignored because, the next morning when the Reading Teacher came into the room and beamed out warmly and smiled lovingly and said to the children, "Let's close our eyes and think of all the happy things that we have to be grateful for and all of the wonderful things that we have been given in our school," it would not do if, at that moment, a child should be wondering about a falling blackboard or a collapsing ceiling or maybe even opening up one eye ever so briefly to make sure that nothing sharp was flying at her head. So that click of denial. A moment later, all that I could see was that the children looked embarrassed. It was the same as with the window the time that it had blown in above their heads. They were embarrassed for the sake of the teacher and for the sake of the school. Embarrassed for the teacher: for her awkwardness and momentary self-accusation. Embarrassed for the school: because this was the only school they had been given and so they had to try to believe with all their heart and soul it was okay.

The girl whose desk was underneath the blackboard now had the most curious expression on her face. I couldn't tell whether it was simply the look of being numb or whether she was not, like so many other of the children in this building, getting herself set up for the introjecting ritual of blaming *herself*. Was she saying with those eyes which looked down so steadily, as if with apology, that she really felt very sorry and did not mean to have gotten her small head in the way of the board? There had been that other little girl, Myra Ann, who had raised her hand one morning, in the midst of reading class, and pleaded up at me from her tiny minnow's face: "Please. Mr. Kozol, I'm trying as hard as I can but I just can't even hear a word you say." Why didn't this little girl get angry? Why couldn't she figure out who or what there was to blame? It is for the same reason that so few of the children ever dreamed of complaining of a teacher and why even the pupils of a teacher who visibly hated and vocally derided the grease of their hair and the color of their skin still would feel grateful for the few scraps of friendship that he managed to drop them on his way. Incorporating the school's structural inadequacies into their own consciousness and attributing to themselves the flaws which the building or the system contained, seemed to be the conditioned reflex of far too many children: gratitude for small goodness, and parental horror of Athenian dimensions at the thought of questioning the ways the gods have ordered things within the Boston Public Schools.

About once a month, it seemed, one child would suddenly and miraculously burst free. It always astonished me. One boy, called out of a Fourth Grade classroom to be rebuked for something by the Principal, got mad at her and told her something she usually didn't hear.

"What can be the matter with you?" she was saying to him.

"Why aren't you grateful for what we have been doing?"

"How can you behave so badly when your teacher is trying so hard to help you and when you know that you have one of the most dedicated teachers in the school?"

And other questions of that sort.

The boy being reprimanded, according to a teacher who was present, suddenly began glaring at her in her snug perch as if he had all at once gotten the idea to chop her up and he yelled at her: "How in Hell do you know anything about it when you weren't even there?" He added, with inspiration: "All that you do is sit here in the office on your fat ass all day long!"

Nobody told me exactly what the Principal said to the student after that, or whether she had him sent down for a whipping that would be equal to the one that she had just received. But I do know that it must have appealed to a common feeling of silent hatred and secret rebellion at the school, because the same story was passed along to me, variously altered and with considerable satisfaction, by a number of teachers for several days after it happened. And I got the feeling that it was something that any number of other people in the school would have liked a lot to say. It was repeated about as often by teachers as by children. Each person changed the words a little bit but the heart of it remained essentially the same: Somebody had gotten good and mad for a change and, unbelievably, told somebody else what he actually thought about something.

The boy in question was the same who had asked me whether there was something called a dry martini. He also was a boy whose jaw had been slashed quite badly with a piece of broken glass in the hand of one of the older children not long before. Both before and after that event, he was being given the rattan regularly by a number of teachers, and he had already something like a slow and steadily searing revolution gradually burning in his eyes. The look— most hated at our school as well as in most black school buildings, because it means that he is getting wised up and, as the School Superintendent has put it, is likely to become an "unmanageable" adult—was the look which is translated into words by the Freedom song "Ain't Gonna Let Nobody Turn Me Round." The boys who manifest this attitude most clearly in segregated classrooms are the ones of whom teachers say, "We haven't been able to quite reach that boy yet." You deeply pray that they won't. I have the feeling, dangerous as it may seem to many people, that it is within the defiant gaze of a boy like that, far sooner than in the down-regarding eyes of a hard-working and obedient student, that the surest help and soonest salvation of his people is going to lie.

The time the blackboard broke and fell provided a clear example of the "obedient" reaction. After the moment of stun was over, the blackboard was righted. One of the custodians was sent for. He came up, inept and disliking the children, a sour mushroom person who told jokes in the cellar about "jigs" and "niggers" and who spoke to me endlessly about the children who wrote on walls, broke windows, stole and broke in and jimmied doors. He came up now because he had to and he fiddled around with the blackboard for a minute or two, said that we shouldn't "turn it so much," and then went away. I thought maybe it was okay, even though he had spent so little time. But the next day it started to sway and topple just the same. We got him up again after a week and this time, with hammer and screws and scrap lumber, he made the thing stand straight. He didn't repair it properly, however, and he gave no promise that it was going to be replaced. He did what slum landlords do when pressed. He used scrap junk that he happened to have around to make a repair that wouldn't cost anything but would silence complaints for a period of time. A social worker who came up to school to talk about a child around that time took a look around our auditorium, I remember, at the scrap lumber-bits, peeled paint, torn curtains, cardboard windows and said to me in disappointment:

"It's exactly like the worst houses in which the poorest of them live."

So now the custodian did nothing except screw on an irregular sawed-off piece of lumber. A month later I turned the board for a science lesson and it cracked suddenly and started to collapse all over. The janitor appeared sourly an hour later and he said that this time he didn't think he would bother to fix it because the thing was "no damn good anyway." After that, it was pushed into a corner and leaned against a wall and we no longer tried to use it. We had three blackboards now, instead of four.

The little girl who had had the near miss with the blackboard was the daughter of a minister. A few days after the accident the minister and his wife came up to school. They did not speak of the accident. They came about another and, seemingly, far less important matter. My memory is that they were speaking about a torn briefcase and about another child's having teased their daughter. While they were talking, however, and for no apparent reason, the mother started weeping. The Reading Teacher, who was present, seemed startled by this outburst and drew no association between this and the recent blackboard incident. I found it hard to believe they had not heard of it. When the mother stopped weeping, the point was made by the Reading Teacher that this little girl actually was not so much teased by other kids as she was something of a troublemaker herself. It happened that this was not the truth but, even if it had been, I did not think it of much importance beside the incident of the blackboard, of which nothing was said at all. The Reading Teacher then delivered an excellent and persuasive assessment of the little girl's incorrect behavior and she was so persuasive that the child ended up by apologizing to the Reading Teacher for all of the things that she had done wrong.

I think this must be classic in Boston, for I have heard of it happening in so many different schools. The parents come up with a just and proper reason to place blame, and they *get* it instead. Up they come angry and with proper outrage. Off they go, humbled, sad and weakly, having as it were apologized for the stupid thing they've tried to obtain. The look of embarrassed humility. The terrible parental horror that they might have made a bad mistake. Will their child now get punished? Will some kind of silent retaliation now take place? What right had they to complain? Wasn't it stupid? Wasn't it unwise of them when they were being received with so much politeness by one of the most respected old-time teachers in the city? The Reading Teacher was brilliant at conveying to Negro parents an earnest kind of persuasive concern and sense of her own absolute moral superiority when it came to a matter of the welfare of their children. She did not display one ounce of meanness. She was solid, kindly, decent. Yet it still was they, not the school authorities, but the parents, who in the end found themselves apologizing for what they had been persuaded to conceive of as their own child's mistake.

The first time we spoke of that child and of her father, the Reading Teacher assured me that the father was not a real minister anyway but that he was a fake. She said without hesitation that she could tell about this from having looked over the records carefully and also from quite a few years' experience in sizing up parents and in knowing what they were like. These helpless statements of condescension on her part frequently would be hemmed around with exaggerated assurances about how many truly fine and truly cultured parents there were in Roxbury. "Mrs. Laramy, for example . . . And little Eleanor's mother . . . A wonderful person! One of the finest human beings that I have ever known." But here was this one case and here was this one assessment: The man in question was no minister and she had proof of that and knew as a matter of fact that actually he worked on a boat, was a sailor or something ordinary like that. If it had been true, then what made me angry was that she did not think what share she and I as white people had had in making such deceptions necessary. And again, if it had been true, the thing that was a hundred times more true was that she as a white woman needed for some reason to think of him as a fake anyway and did not really like the idea of his possible distinction as a minister but took a vocal and somehow juicy kind of relish and satisfaction in getting across to me the idea that he was a pretender:

"He's no minister. I can tell you that for certain. I don't know where he got that piece of cloth but he's an obvious fake. They can set up a pulpit in a store room and he'll stand up in front of them and pray."

But of course the thing that is most important and most devastating in this case is that it was *not* true, for the man was very much a minister, and happened to be a quite distinguished one. It also happens that he had held a salaried position in the U.S. Navy in order to earn some extra money, and it was upon this fact, I believe, that the Reading Teacher was basing her derogating statement.

Minister or sailor, however, and whether he had been an ordinary deck hand or the captain of the ship, within two months of that conversation tragedy was to strike his family. The man's wife died in childbirth and the newborn child died as well. Charlene now was motherless. The Reading Teacher, with strong instincts of motherhood and kindliness, instantly galvanized herself into action and did some traditional, benevolent good deeds. A visit to the home. Special attention to the child. Assurances to the father. And a number of similar actions: all kindly and substantial and apparently honest and worthwhile. She, the Art Teacher and the Math Teacher went together to the funeral. I asked if I could go also but was not permitted to do so, for

there would not have been anybody left to stay with
the children. The delegation went in any case and,
when they returned, the Reading Teacher astonished
me by being all in giggles. The change in her was
remarkable. Whether it was due to the two hours'
company of the Art and Math Teachers, or whether
it was due to some real intrinsic shift in her feelings,
I did not know. But her whole tone was different.
From an attitude of generosity, warm feeling and
motherly goodness, she now had shifted into a mood
of high hilarity. She had to confess to me, she said,
all excited (and in a manner that she adopted very
often, as if not merely I but whoever else she was
talking to would inevitably agree) that "the whole
thing was so embarrassing and so ridiculous" that
she and the Art Teacher and the Math Teacher
had had all they could do "not to laugh right out
loud right there in the place." I remembered plenty
of occasions on which she had condemned those two,
even ridiculed them, for the kind of malice that she
now was sharing. She had condemned them severely
—in the same way that she spoke of other people—
yet now she went to the funeral with them and returned to tell me that "it wasn't even like a funeral.
It was like a jazz program. They had a singer
there who was just like Eartha Kitt. Children were
screaming and running all around the place and they
passed out fans and even printed up a program and
had nurses all around in case anyone should faint."

I said: "You mean it was like a revival meeting?"

"It was so primitive!" was what the Reading Teacher
said.

Then she said, once again with apparent kindness
and reflection and with a sense of obligation which
was no longer humorous or consciously derogatory
in the least but absolutely serious and severe: "I
see, after that, what we all have to work against
in school and how far we have to go to reach those
children."

She said to me also: "It's true, I suppose, that some of our funerals would seem offensive to other people too."

But she added right after that: "I think that everyone who teaches Negro children in this kind of school ought to go to a Negro funeral at least once, just in order to know the kinds of things he has to work against."

Obviously, I have no idea what kind of funeral it actually was; it may, for all I know, have been the most conservative funeral on earth. But I cannot believe that any funeral—of whatever sort—could be of instructive use or value to a teacher whose mind was so filled with senseless bigotry. And, because of the Reading Teacher's remark about primitive emotion, I thought again of something that I had thought about before: about the kinds of relatively safe and bland values that the Reading Teacher and many other white teachers like her were seeking endlessly to spread upon the Negro children's heads. I thought that Charlene and the other Negro children in the school ought to start praying God for help right now if any of these women had the idea of trying to replace the good things the children had already with the kinds of things that they thought were worthwhile. The Reading Teacher also told me that "the better class of people there were embarrassed to have us see it." And I thought that possibly they were, but then that would only have been to their own dishonor—for I believed that the people whom the Reading Teacher meant by "the better people" were very likely those who had the least satisfaction in being Negro and who might have wished the most to be like her. I never did get over a sense of astonishment at the joke the Reading Teacher brought back from the funeral that day and the way she assumed that I would share it with her.

TEN

IN the middle of the winter Mrs. Hicks was returned by her fellow committee members to the position she had just vacated as chairman of the Boston School Committee. As she was re-elected she referred to the problem that we were facing in these words: "I don't think we have to concern ourselves with the Negro issue. We have given them everything they asked for."

About a month later there was an annual convention of school superintendents in Atlantic City. Boston's hired school Superintendent, William Ohrenberger, a man chosen and held in power by the elected School Committee, attended the conference in order to represent our school system. The following item was sent back and printed in the Boston *Globe*:

In Atlantic City . . . school administrators from across the nation gathered for their annual confab and tossed around the critical issues facing the public school systems today . . . Urban school problems were given much attention and the first major panel of the meeting was on de facto segregation. What emerged was of unique relevance to Boston. It was pointed out that Boston was the only city in the United States that anyone had heard of where school officials actually voted that there wasn't any de facto segregation. In the South, the de jure segregation of the past has been readily admitted, and even lauded, by segregationists. In northern urban areas, de facto segregation stemming essentially from residential ghettoes has again and again been noted by school officials, even though little has been done to make a major breakthrough to dissolve this pattern. But Boston stands alone in saying officially and unequivocally that no such condition exists here.

Two weeks later, on the first Monday of March, I had an opportunity to go in town to visit an evening meeting of the Boston School Committee. Although I was not apt by any means to be an impartial observer of the proceedings, it still seemed of value to me to visit and to observe this meeting and I was anxious to form an opinion for myself of the five-man group and of their Superintendent. The School Committee sat behind a low closed railing. A press table was set up a little beneath them. An audience heavily weighted with Negro people was seated out in front. Of the five members of the committee, Mrs. Hicks was seated in the center. On one side of her were Thomas Eisenstadt and Joseph Lee. On the other, after the Superintendent, were William O'Connor and Arthur Gartland. I thought Eisenstadt looked like a clever nimble person. He gave the impression of a perky little high school speaking champ who had just won his first debate. O'Connor seemed sere, dull, gloomy, inconspicuous. Gartland seemed dignified and intelligent, a man in his fifties or sixties, quiet-seeming and quietly wise. Mrs. Hicks seemed more comical than I had expected, an earnest and tremendous squeaking person. Mr. Lee seemed a gentleman, but senescent, and a gentleman from quite another, distant age. Ohrenberger, the Superintendent, was in many ways the most disappointing one of all.

Perhaps there was little reason for high expectation of Ohrenberger, since his public utterances, or those that I had seen, could not have given one a high impression of the man, and they were in fact

more likely than not to have achieved the opposite
effect. Those beliefs that he had been willing to im-
part to print had made it clear that the man had only
the most lukewarm idea of the realities of social
change or prejudice, and no idea at all of the
degree to which he himself was sustaining and nour-
ishing that prejudice by his own words and deeds.
I received the impression, in Ohrenberger, of a man
who lived in fear that he might have very few intellectual capabilities, yet who felt it was incumbent
upon himself as Superintendent to try to talk in
the manner in which he believed that a superintendent ought to talk. He seemed greatly ill at ease in
a world of polysyllables or of unsimplified ideas,
yet he insisted upon using the former in order to try
to get across the latter, the result of this being
that neither word nor content ever sounded real.
Despite these things, my father had known Ohrenberger as a young man in Boston when they had
been students and he often had spoken of him affec-
tionately. I therefore believed that in person he
might come across somehow as a more dedicated or
more interesting man than he had seemed in print.
But this proved not to be true.

Watching the Superintendent that evening and then
putting his immediate presence against what was
known of him, it was difficult to know whether to
blame the man for the administration or the administration for the man. He appeared, with his hoarse-
voiced style and plodding manner, to be far less
of an actual school administrator than the carica-
ture of a school principal on television. One had to
remind oneself that this man was no television principal but the top man in the entire Boston system.
It is difficult to imagine many other communities in
the United States or Europe that would tolerate
something like this happening when it came to the
matter of the administration of their schools. The
whole idea of a good-hearted football coach being

in a position to run an entire system of public schools
in an age and in an hour when even a brilliant
statesman or deeply prepared scholar would have
been hard put to know which way to turn seems to
belong to some kind of farce-drama. The farce, however, is not drama: it is a system of real-life teachers, children, schools.

The Superintendent did not say much the night
that I was at the School Committee, but reading his
previous statements, his apologetic or defensive writings, had always seemed to me much like being jerked
and jolted over every large idea. There would appear occasionally, in his talk and press releases, hints
and bits of intellectual phrasing. Only it would be
grafted into an overall sound of heaviness and
heart's ineptitude as if an honest speech-writer had
done everything he could to get it to sound right
but had only half-succeeded in the job. Perhaps
there is some danger in speaking in this manner
about anybody at all because there always may be
areas in which a man is more capable than anyone
has ever guessed and which he has never permitted
the public to suspect. But Ohrenberger seemed to me
that evening, frankly, a nice person of extremely
modest competence who somehow had gotten himself into a lucrative position for which he knew he
was not fitted.

The night that I was at the School Committee,
the parents of the overcrowded Endicott District
of Roxbury had come up to make a formal complaint about conditions at their school. Instead of
being allowed to speak or make presentations, however, they were forced to sit through two hours of
discussion having nothing to do with them, and
then were insulted by being kept waiting through
an interminable and seemingly unnecessary pause.
After that pause they still were not allowed to speak
but were obliged instead to sit through an insulting
speech delivered to the School Committee, but ad-

dressed in a certain sense to them, by Joseph Lee. The speech was a potpourri of unconscious racism and naïveté, interlaced with platitudes and professions of good feeling. The reason this speech seems important to me is because of the way it reflected things that were being said in school—only stating them more bluntly—and also because of the comments that were made about this speech by the Reading Teacher when we talked about it the following day at school.

Joseph Lee's speech of March 3, 1965, is printed in the back part of this book. The details from the speech which stand out in my mind have to do mostly with the kind of language that he used. It seems important to remember that this speech was given, not in closed session to a group of his peers or associates, but to a large and crowded audience of Negro ministers, Negro parents and their friends. Lee's main effort was to demonstrate how futile and how hopeless any serious efforts at educational integration were certain to be. His argument was that moving Negro children outside the ghetto would defeat itself as a method of integration because the Negroes would soon move outside the ghetto classrooms in such numbers that once again, wherever the Negroes went, they would outnumber the white people. The feeling Lee conveyed and by which he appeared to be deeply alarmed was the fear of a horde that would, in its tribal movement, prove inexorable, drowning out all safe islands of white ascendancy and turning Boston into a predominantly black town. The terms "settlement," "influx," "heartland" and "population take-over" remain memorable among the words he used. He also employed, to the embarrassment of many people present, the image of a "cleansing fluid" used to try to rid a pair of trousers of their stain. The cleansing fluid was equated with plans of integration: the stain with the Negro. The Negro majority, said Lee, moving out from the ghetto center, was like the stain of blackness on a child's pants. The precise words he used were "the mark on the knee of a child's breeches when he falls on a tarry schoolyard or street." This was not very far from saying that a little Negro child *was* in fact the tar on the white schoolyard and that to accept this little boy into a formerly white school was to endanger the cleanliness of *everybody's* pants. Moreover, said Lee, the movement of the Negro child out of the ghetto center would not be successful and this, he indicated, was true for the same reason that the cleansing fluid does not really clean the pants. All that it does is to spread the dirt out a little bit more evenly so that you do not see it as a single spot. "The cleansing fluid will relieve the mark all right," he said. "But the mark will just re-appear as a ring on the cloth . . ."

I can't say whether or not this is true about the use of cleansing fluid, but such words as a metaphor for integration could hardly have failed to be in-sulting to Negro mothers and fathers. Some of the people who heard it looked as though they had been slapped. Others looked as if they would like to kick him in the face. Lee looked out over his half-moon glasses almost like a childish madman. He stared at the Negro mothers and Negro fathers and Negro ministers and he said to them things which even a secret racist oughtn't to have had the nerve to say behind their backs. Many things he said were unpleasant but perhaps the most shocking was a two- or three-minute dissertation which he delivered on the high reproduction rate of Negro women. "Populations change," he began, fairly innocently. But then he veered off into a crazy matrix of mathe-matical figures and geometrical progressions which seemed to herald the possibility of an all-black Bos-ton or all-black America within another 100 years. He said that Negro women were producing children more than twice as fast as white women. For this reason, he seemed to believe, America and Boston were doomed to race-inundation.

"In other words," he said, getting up steam for an extraordinary diatribe, "if the white population of America is to stay about the same, and the Negro population is to double with each generation under its present high birthrate, then the *10* Negro units in every present 100 units of American population will become *20* Negro units with the next generation 20 years from now; then it will become *40* Negro units in the second generation 40 years from now; in the third generation *80* units 60 years from now; and *160* units 80 years from now—while the white population remains static at 90 units . . ." Lee said that if a young man such as Mr. Eisenstadt lived to a good old age, he would see America "a predominantly Negro nation, like Africa." He added to this that "the population take-over by Negroes" would come "much sooner in the big warm-hearted cities like Boston than in the cold-blooded suburbs . . ."

Lee also pointed out to the Negro people sitting in the room that their neighborhood (Roxbury) was actually a great deal more isolated and separated from his own neighborhood (Boston proper) than they had known. "Only recently," he said, "was today's overwhelmingly Negro Roxbury hitched to Boston. Many people now living can remember Roxbury as a small country town, under its own selectmen, connected to Boston by a narrow isthmus . . . Suppose Roxbury had never been engrossed into Boston. It would then have its own Negro government, its Negro police force, its own schools—to its own liking. Would it then accuse itself of racial discrimination? any more than the all-Negro schools of the new Negro nations of Africa? or the all-Negro and Negro-governed towns in the South and Southwest? Or would it be so accused by others? Is the accident of political jurisdiction, or inclusion in a larger municipality, the matter of irritation?

Roxbury is separated from part of Boston by part of the Atlantic ocean, with no bridge between . . . Is it realistic," he asked therefore, "to make past political gerrymandering the determining factor in fuming at Boston's racial life . . . ?"

The parents who had left their children tonight and come all the way into town at seven and sat through two hours of tedium and of argumentation and an hour of recess, and many of whom had been rudely insulted downstairs before the elevators by an unnecessary and uncustomary ad hoc rule to let no more than two people into the elevator at any one time, these parents whose only wish was to get some desks and teachers for their children in a school that would be properly set up to teach them before another year of schooling had gone completely by the board, had to sit now and listen to Mr. Lee telling them, essentially, to get back and stay back in Roxbury and leave his clean and old and white and Yankee Boston to its own. Even this was not enough. He went further before he was done. From geography he swung around again to biology and to the high reproduction rate of Negro women. "A fraction of Boston girls," said Lee, "bear children one after another, sired by stray men who don't stay around— with an increase of pay from public alms for every new child. A Gallup survey of New York shows that approximately ⅔ of the 1,000 children born to persons on relief every month enter this world without the benefit of marriage between their parents. The Boston percentage is probably not much less. It does not help a girl to be honorable to pay her with public funds to be the reverse. Disbursements by taxedly charitable Boston to mothers for no-marriage-bells children already are 3 million dollars a year . . . How are our schools to supply a needed father-image in teaching such half-homed and half-backed children? . . ."

He then gave the following brief historical summary, which could have come straight out of one of our most mediocre and antiquated texts. His effort to be kindly about it and to show understanding are the things that seem so tragic. At school the Reading Teacher made fun of him later and said that he was crazy, but I did not think that there was a great deal of distance between the things that he said and many things that she believed. When she said that he was crazy I think that what she really meant was that he was crazy to shoot off his mouth so openly when a more discreet white man would have known enough to keep it shut. These were his words:

"As to the morality of re-allocating tax-raised funds (which, otherwise, are creating a permanent leisure class—lolling in idleness on the backs of the toiling masses—out of both whites and Negroes such as take for granted a continual tax-furnished dole as a way of life) it is argued sometimes as a special condonement for dependence on public aid by occasional Negro-Americans up from the South, here among them, that such Negro-Americans are justly resentful and excusable victims of the ravages and immorality of past slavery. This is important for white citizens to remember. As for matrimony, Negro marriages were seldom allowed under Southern slavery, and unmarried motherhood was the imposed and accepted code. The unconsenting and unrequited Negro girl, too, served the immoral white man's pleasure. It is no worse for the Negro to flout the whole white race because of some bad experiences in the past than for a white man to decry the whole Negro race because of some poor samples."

He then went on to exonerate from all responsibility any of the white people, descendants of Yankees or any others, living in Boston at the present time. ". . . For actuality," Lee said, "no young or old Negro-American today has been a slave. Besides, almost the whole population of Boston is made up of persons of Irish, Italian, Polish, Canadian, and Jewish background, who were miles away from America at the time of slavery. If a few Yankees still live in Boston, their grandsires atoned for the sins of their race by shedding their blood in the 4-year horror of Civil War battlefields. Greater love hath no man than this, that he lay down his life for his friends." The reason for saying this (on Lee's part), I suppose, was to do again what the history books did: to say that nobody in America really did anything wrong, nobody alive now needs to have a bad conscience, and we live in a pretty fair, square and democratic land. But this is not true. We do not live in such a land. And it is an odd thing to say at a moment and in a country in which so many people are wracked by bad conscience as by no other mental or physical disease. Lee managed to exonerate everybody. Who then was to blame? If nobody, then there could be no cause for blame. There could be nothing really wrong. This, of course, was what the Boston School Committee had been saying all year long.

When the Reading Teacher had said once that I was being cynical, or trying to teach cynicism, she was probably right about it to this extent: that I did feel suspicious and do feel suspicious of my own motives and of those of most other white people. Perhaps that is one reason why I could not help feeling suspicious when I heard Mr. Lee winding up his talk to the Negro parents in these words: "Every American—Negro-American or otherwise—can and should live on the lessons of the past. No one should live within the past. It is no good to duck the lively present for a dead past." He then said this: "The predominantly Chinese schools in the heart of Boston, with their crack regiments of scholars, or the predominantly corpse-colored, Yankee schools of Wellesley, with their tolerable scholars, feel no loss of hope and prospect by reason of their scholars' studying desk to desk beside only their own kin and kind. Would it not be better," he asked, "to plant the road to a rewarded future so firmly in the minds of our Negro elementary school children in their present, specially-instructed neighborhood schools that they can proceed into racially well diversified Junior High and High School with every sense of the worth of themselves and confidence in their competence to meet life's problems? Rather than attempt external shifts and transportational changes, resented by Negro parents, would it not be better to give our Negro pupils a change of heart? And that is exactly what the Boston Schools in their enormous and uncrumpling devotion to their Negro pupils are trying to do."

A Negro lady sitting at the School Committee meeting that night said to me later: "I didn't come all the way in town to listen to that. I could have read it in old books. All I wanted was to get my child into a school with a teacher and some chairs."

It is not hard to imagine how she felt. For all Mr. Lee's words, and all his protestation, and all the Victorian elegance and elaboration of his language, the children in the Endicott classrooms still would not have desks and chairs to sit on the next morning, and none of his well-intended polysyllables had brought the hour of their relief and vindication a moment nearer. Bitterness in the Roxbury community was measurably higher after that evening, and I felt my own attitudes considerably changed from that point on. I could not sleep that night, and the next day I taught poorly and had a hard time getting through the morning. It was because the feelings that had been evinced during those three hours up on the crest of Beacon Hill had seemed not merely prejudice but a willful refusal to encounter head-on the real situation that was faced every day by many thousands of young children There was no affiliation between the things that Mr. Lee went on about and the way that the urine and coal-dust smelled down in the basement of my school

There was no connection, either, between Miss Sullivan's statements in the press about her dedicated teachers and the man at my school who took such relish and satisfaction in explaining to me the intricacies of whipping or the three female teachers who went off to the funeral of a Negro mother and came back laughing. I thought after that night, which marked the end of winter and the beginning of a new feeling in me, that Mr. Lee had not spoken merely for himself as a lonely eccentric but had spoken for our city and had gotten absolutely to the well-meaning core of the lack of democracy within our public schools.

ELEVEN

If Mr. Lee's words seemed at a distance from reality, the reality remained, as always, back at school. In the end of winter, or just as spring approached, a whole series of events began to bring changes to our school, although few were for the better. One of them had to do with Stephen.

I have said before that one of the most appealing things about this boy was the pleasure that he took in drawing. Some of his pictures told freely and exactly what was on his mind. He drew lovely lyrical cows and pleasant horses lifting up their hooves to rub their noses, and a bird lost alone upon a weirdly slanting geometric rooftop, and a large hunched rabbit, its ears alert for danger, in a colossal and uniform woods. One day a little before Christmas he had handed me another folded crumpled picture at a moment when he thought nobody looked. At home I opened up the paper. It was a childishly detailed picture of a Christmas living room as it is shown in typical cheerful books and in it there were a Christmas tree and toys and a mantelpiece and everything that you would expect to see and also this: one beautiful tall lovely-haired good fairy holding out a twinkling wand above the head of a sad-eyed little child. One did not have to go terribly far to see in this drawing a picture of the mother of whom he had dreamed repeatedly, but whom he had in fact not ever seen, coming at last to grant him the wish he might have asked, perhaps no more than that she knew him and would love him and would take care of him, so that he could actually exist with safety in his own mind once again. Or possibly something more practical and immediate and tangible than that: a toy that he wanted perhaps, a kite or a pencil-set or a sled. Whatever he meant, it was a sad enough and obvious enough wish. And then there would be no mother coming. There would be no good fairy and no magic wand. There would be no father either, although there might be a weary and over-burdened social worker who would come with a few presents marked "From Santa." And that was it.

Nobody, as Mr. Lee would have been the first to say and as the Reading Teacher frequently reminded me, could have blamed the school for this. If you believed in the innate rottenness of certain human beings, you could blame the child and you could say, as it was said at school almost daily or somebody, that he was just plain miserable and no good. Or, if you were more combative and realistic you could blame the State Division of Child Guardianship which was responsible for placing him in a dangerous home, for not looking after his mental health and for taking no interest in the fact that he went uneducated with no permanent teachers for two years in a hapless morbid school. You couldn't blame the school for all that. But you could blame the school for this:

When these things were noticed, observed, thought about, the school discouraged you, by a policy which seemed to militate carefully against Negro children, from doing anything about it. I've said already that the Reading Teacher ran into no opposition when she did a number of favors for white children—arranging summer camp for one child, giving another one a present, having the parents of a third child come to her home. Who would have objected to modest favors of this sort? For they were normal human actions. Yet I have demonstrated that every act which

I attempted of a similar nature and which happened to have involved a Negro child was either tacitly discouraged or else explicitly forbidden.

Frederick, for example, had gradually made regular the practice of waiting for me outside the schoolhouse at two-thirty and he would then confide to me things that were disturbing him as I gave him the short ride to his home, not three blocks off. After a time the Reading Teacher commented to me that he was behaving better and she also observed how much of his resentfulness was gone. I liked being with him and I drove him home selfishly because it was fun to be able to chat with a student outside of school when the discipline panic which prevailed during school hours was no longer in effect. There was a chance suddenly to find out who a student might actually be as soon as he did not have to be designated as so much teachable or unteachable material sitting in such and such a row and such and such a chair. I did not find that dropping him home caused me any trouble with him at school. He still did the work he was asked to do, only somewhat better than before, and he still treated me with respect. Yet, in regard to this friendship with him, I soon was given the following advice:

(1) To have any friendly relationship with a student outside the classroom would make teaching him impossible or, at the least, substantially more difficult. To know him as he is and to allow him to know you in any ordinary vulnerable light is likely to affect adversely both the way in which you think of him and the way in which he thinks of you.

(2) It is dangerous to a student for you to have any contact with him outside of school. No matter what the danger may be of his being entirely lost, ignored and stifled within the general oblivion of a dismal segregated school, the danger of his being in a traffic accident with you if you drive him three blocks home represents a greater danger.

(3) To show any affection for a student, as by driving him home or buying him a gift or giving him advice about something unconnected to school, may easily place the teacher himself in a great deal of danger and may well subject him to accusations of an unsavory kind. The prime accusation about which I was given warning was that of a parent or onlooker who might wonder why a man, a normal man, at any rate, should take such a peculiar interest in a child. "You never want one of them alone," was the way one teacher said it to me. "Protect yourself ahead of time. You never know what somebody may think."

The Principal said: "You must not take the risk of driving a child home, even though I believe your own motives are good."

The Reading Teacher said: "It was thoughtful of you to give Stephen a Christmas present. But you will learn later on that you cannot teach them if you are going to be in the position of a friend."

The Supervisor who came out to observe and grade me for the School Department gave me this advice as well: "You are here to keep order and to teach these children, not to be a pal to every passing boy. PAL, as a matter of fact," he said, "stands for the Police Athletic League. You should remember that you're here to instruct them and keep them orderly, not to be a big brother."

One day in March Stephen came up to my desk, sidled against it, and whispered very softly in my ear. I have said that he weighed only sixty pounds.

"Can I ask you just one question?"

"Yes," I said.

He looked way down at the floor. At last he whispered with great embarrassment that what was upsetting him was a word that he had heard. He was at that time nine years old. Would I tell him what the word meant if he told me what it was? I said that I would. He looked down at the floor again, scuffled his feet some more, looked up and said, "But it's nasty." And when he said it he seemed much younger than he was.

I said, "It's okay. You can tell me. I won't tell anybody else." But he suddenly lost what courage he had had and just wandered off.

A little later, without warning, he was in front of me again. "You promise you won't tell anyone?" he said. I promised him again. Desperately, as if something terrible were about to happen, he bit his mouth and whispered: "INTERCOURSE." He said it like that, as if it were the largest word in the world, and then he looked down, horrified and panicky, at his sneakers pointed together on the floor. I asked him where he had heard it and he said, "From my mother." That was the foster mother with whom he had been placed.

"Did she tell you?"

He said: "Yes."

"Then you know that it isn't nasty."

"Isn't it?"

I said: "You know it's not."

"No, I don't." He had a soft little voice. And still he would not lift up his eyes from their firm focus on the floor.

"What did your mother say?"

"She said that that's how babies are born."

"Then you know that it's not a nasty thing. Who is it who tried to tell you that?"

"Mr. Kozol?" he said suddenly, looking up at me with complete frankness all at once: "Does that mean that that's how I was born and how everybody was?"

"That's how everyone was born."

He looked embarrassed when I said it, but genuinely gratified, and then he shuffled off without a single word more. He went along, in one of his reveries, to his pathetic little desk, always looking at his own feet, and crumpled himself back down into his chair. Later that day he came and asked me

my first name. I told him what it was and he said,
"I never heard of it" and when I told him how to
spell it and where it came from, he wandered away
and did not ask about it after that.

At times like that, when he seemed so cut off from
the other children, the only real breaks in his silence would be when he would come up to say something minor but confidential in my ear or else when
he would suddenly, and completely irrationally,
make a rude interruption in the middle of a class.
There also were moments when he really seemed to
be having a conversation either with himself or
with another person whom I could not observe. I
once heard him saying out loud in the middle of a
class: "I'm Hercules. I'm a king. I'm the strongest
person in the world." He was the littlest and weakest
boy in the whole class. His life, already difficult, was
made desolate at school. Outside of school it seemed
that he sometimes became a full human being again.
That was one reason why I took the opportunities
available to see him outside of school. The difference
between the real child and the child in the chair at
school was immense in all cases. It was the difference,
specifically, between somebody artificial and somebody real. But in the case of Stephen there was the
greatest difference of all.

During the first good spring weekend, I took
Stephen and another boy from school, and an old
summer pupil of mine from the tutoring classes,
over to Cambridge and then out to the country for a
while. A female friend of mine who had a child of
her own came with us in order to make it more fun
and to give me some help. My pupil from the summer was a slightly older boy and he assumed, without my asking him, the part of an older brother to
the younger children. His kindness and protective-
ness to Stephen were quite noticeable, for he
recognized clearly—with his shrewdness and unselfish
nature—that this was a person who had to go through

life with many troubles. And the entire time was satisfying, although so many things about Stephen's life made all of us feel sad.

Most saddening of all was how grateful he appeared for everything that he was given. It was as if he had never gotten a penny or a grain of sand for nothing in his life. All the talk in school was of how you had to earn everything. You could not breathe air, have peace, laugh or smile or hope ever to equal a white man without having first piled up vast credits to your account within the Boston Public Schools. When Stephen spent the day with us in Cambridge and in the country he was an endlessly thankful guest. The lady who came with us to help me remarked later about how gentle and self-effacing he seemed. All afternoon I noticed that she kept looking at him with the look that mothers have for their own children. When we asked him if he wanted tonic at lunchtime, instead of saying yes, he asked me if he could have a cup of tea. He had his tea, with sugar and milk, and then asked after a while if he could have some more. If the sound of this is rather Dickensian, perhaps the association is not a bad one; for there was much in Stephen's life and the Boston School system reminiscent of the things that Dickens wrote about. The degree to which Stephen appeared to feel gratitude for the ordinary fun we had that day seemed overwhelming. He spoke about that afternoon for days to come. At school once a few weeks later, when he had been quiet and distant for a certain while, he came up to me and asked me privately if I would ever again take him over to visit at the home of the lady in Cambridge who had been so nice to him. I said that I didn't think it could be possible so long as we were still in school, but I promised him I would take him there again as soon as school was over. He seemed greatly satisfied by that promise and every so often afterward he came up and whispered in my ear: "I can't wait until June."

There is nothing unusual about any of these happenings. They ought to be normal and ordinary. What is special is that they were forbidden. What is special is that they were considered to militate unfortunately against teacher separation and teacher autocracy and were considered to be a threat to the discipline structure of a segregated school. Keeping a teacher from being a friend to a child enabled the teacher to deny for his own comfort the complicated nature of every person of any kind who is alive. It was easy enough to think of a child as "such and such a fellow, with glasses, fairly quiet, in row five." Then one day you looked up and, prompted by something that had been in the text, you asked him suddenly: "David, what does your father do?" And the answer that time, from a real David, with glasses, told you something suddenly that you had never known of him before and something that made his solemnity understandable and made his whole uniqueness very much alive:

"My father's dead, Mr. Kozol."

It was in much the same way that I would suddenly sit up and really take a special look at Stephen, as he came up to my desk and whispered very gently and very timidly to me that he couldn't "wait until June." June, of course, in the sense that Stephen meant it, was not going to come.

During March and April, according to notes I scribbled down, Stephen became progressively more withdrawn and was—without my knowledge—given a beating by a teacher once again. This beating followed by several weeks after a time when it had been fully recognized at school that he was seriously disturbed and it came at a moment when he was being given an unusual amount of harassment for many reasons and, as it seemed, from all directions. The order and the sequence of these troubles went somewhat like this:

One day Stephen just walked in and announced to me out of the blue that he was going to be leaving.

He said that he would not be seeing me again. He had been told, he said, to pack all his things because he was going to be moving the next day. Where was he going? The only answer he had gotten was to some kind of home. Someone had told him that it must be a reform school and so he sat all day in tears. He took me aside and told me secretly that he was being "sent away for good." He didn't know where. I asked him how did he know then that he was really going? "Because all my things are packed." It was the same day that he asked me for my telephone number and I wrote it out for him and gave him also several other ways in which he could reach me if he ever wanted and couldn't get me at home. He was in a state of total fear. The Reading Teacher noticed it and felt terrible and treated him with affection, I thought, for almost the first time the whole year. She said to him: "Stephen, I hope you will be happy because I know that you will not want to work or be a good boy until you have a chance at some happiness." And that was so. But the only trouble was: Next day he returned! Something had gone wrong and he wasn't leaving for a few more days. The letdown after the great send-off was terrible. The Reading Teacher got angry and fed up with him all over again. Again I was forbidden to have anything to do with him and so forth, and he found himself trapped once more within the frozen status quo and unmercy of the school.

What had gone wrong, I asked him? How come the social worker had had to change the time? Was he leaving or wasn't he? What was going to happen? The answer to all of these questions was expressed finally in these words: "The social worker called my mother and told her she can't get rid of me because he doesn't know any place where I can go and also she's had me so long she has to keep me. So I have to stay."

I asked: "What about your clothes?"

He said they were going to be unpacked.

It can easily be imagined how terrified and bewildered he must have been by then. The questions raised by these events would have posed for any child the most elemental and overwhelming questions: Was he leaving or wasn't he? Should he pack or shouldn't he? Did any grown-ups know or didn't they? Was there any place anywhere for him—would there ever be?—or wasn't there? Meanwhile, being so assaulted by the State and society in general, he also was getting himself into deeper trouble in his home. His foster mother, it seemed, did not know many ways to deal with him other than by yelling or by beatings. He used to come to school with his little bag of sandwiches and his eyes glued down in horror to the floor. When he looked up I would see the lines of streaked blood from his chin to up above his eyebrows and when I asked him what had happened he would answer always in a shy, evasive tone. I began this book by speaking of a day when finally he came to school with his left cheek and jaw all purple and with his eye all battered. The Reading Teacher and the class together had stared in real alarm when he came in at the door. "What happened?" I had asked him, but at first he wouldn't really answer. All he would say, in an offhand manner, was that he had "bumped" it when somebody had opened up a door.

Later that day I called him over to the corner and he told me in a whisper that his foster mother had accused him of stealing money and then had thrown him out onto the porch. It would not come as a surprise to me if he had stolen some of her money. He got so little in life, was robbed himself of so much in so many ways, was so bitterly taken-away-from, that it would not be any surprise if he should finally—by a gesture of sufficient concreteness—try to steal some of it back. I do not think that he had stolen anything but I would consider it quite understandable and almost natural if he had. Any Negro child who stole anything movable out of any home or Boston schoolhouse would not have stolen back as much as has been stolen from him.

Occasionally after that Stephen would come up to my desk and ask me furtively if I remembered something that I had promised about June. When I said that I did remember he would tell me again that he couldn't wait until June and then he would drop something all crumpled and folded on my desk. Once it was a new picture he had drawn. Once: some more funnies that he had cut out of the newspaper. Once: his telephone number scribbled on a little paper scrap. After that gift (the telephone number) he asked me occasionally: "Did you try to call me up?" I would say that I hadn't. Still, he wanted to be sure that I hadn't lost his number. I said that I had not. I had put it away safe in a drawer.

"Good."

He always said just what he thought. I got to like him as much as any child I've ever known and when his social worker told me that it was hard to find a parent to adopt him I thought that this was difficult to believe and I had to wonder exactly what kinds of parents (white or Negro? rich or poor?) they had in mind. I am certain there are people in the world who would have loved him greatly, and that there are people who would not have found it an overwhelming experience to have had to sustain the burden of his difficulties. For, with all of his troubles, he was a very pleasant, honest, open child. Had the school and State together taken any proper thought or care for his well-being, I am convinced that he would not today be caught up in the trap of fear and sickness but that he would be able to share, no matter with how many reservations, in the blessings that are taken for granted by most children.

TWELVE

MUCH of the news that held the attention of the Boston papers during February and March in 1965 had to do with civil rights. Stories of murder from the South competed for space on the front page with news about the behavior of the Boston School Committee, all of this being given an occasional flourish on the editorial page in a letter to the paper from School Committee member Joseph Lee. The one event which dominated all others, however, was the death in Selma, Alabama, of Reverend Reeb. The reaction to his death, on the part of thousands of Bostonians, was angry and anguished and articulate. A crowd of 30,000 people gathered on a Sunday afternoon in Boston Common to mourn and eulogize this minister, while two hundred young civil rights workers chose to demonstrate their feelings in another way by organizing a massive sit-in at the U.S. Federal Building. Several of the people who rose to speak before the crowd in Boston Common did not hesitate to draw a line of similarity between the events that were then taking place in Alabama and the less bloody but, in the long run, no less destructive processes of injustice that were being carried out within the Boston Public Schools. Possibly I found this connection the more reasonable and more believable because the death of Reverend Reeb coincided almost to the day and week with one of the very deepest periods of withdrawal in Stephen's private life, as well as with one of the most serious periods of difficulty in his life at school. It was also

at the same time, as I have described already, that
the Reading Teacher confided in me, with warm
energy and glowing complacence, that at least it was
wonderful that we could come to school and forget
about what was happening down in Alabama.

That weekend I was having dinner with friends
in Cambridge and I was trying to describe to them
some of the conditions that we faced at school. I
also described to them the struggle I was having to
bring myself up to the point of being truthful and
the hesitation I felt about braving the certain hostility of other teachers at my school if I should be
more forthright. I said, what was the truth, that I
felt compromised by my compliance and in particular that I felt disturbed by the degree to which
I had permitted myself to be appropriated by the
Reading Teacher and the Art Teacher, so that I was
continually being stifled and suppressed precisely at
those moments when I knew it was most imperative
that I speak out.

From talking about my own school, the conversation drifted gradually to the problem in general and
inevitably, to the protest at the Federal Building
that was taking place at that hour. Young people
whom I admired greatly had spent close to thirty
hours unfed and unwashed and sleepless on the
floors of that government building and had refused to
allow police to drive them away. This was the only
way that they could think of to protest our Federal
Government's timidity in defending the lives of
whites and Negroes in the South. A respectable and
ambitious Harvard Law student offered us the information that he considered it all "very young and
immature," and there was not any doubt in my mind
at all that he would indeed have to have found it
young and immature since to approve of it and not
find it immature might well make him feel that he
should be a part of it and to be a part of it might
prejudice his offered job at a leading New York

firm. I said that to him and I also said that I thought the greatest risk those demonstrators were undergoing was not physical harm or physical arrest but rather the sophisticated and supercilious ridicule of people exactly like him. I said that even if they were mostly young and scruffy and beatnik-looking they seemed to me to be the only people in Boston that night who were in visible touch with American reality because they were actually sitting down on the floor of a building that represented federal power. Everybody else was at dinner tables like ourselves discussing the government's inaction. Millions disapproved of the President's hesitation, yet they confined themselves to talk. Only those young SNCC and CORE workers had had the courage to act on what they thought.

Now at night at this comfortable dinner party, after I had said what I did, the law student suddenly questioned me: "If you mean what you said and you really admire them for doing what they have done, then why aren't you right down there with them on the floor instead of sitting here talking about it and enjoying yourself just like the rest of us?" I felt a moment of panic at being put on the spot. And then I got up and said that he was right and I would have to go there. It seems a slight enough thing but it is not always so easy to do that in your own home town if you have grown up caring a great deal about pleasing adult people and when some of the people your family has been closest to are the people who command a large portion of respect. Two other people at the dinner table announced that they were coming with me. In the next three hours the three of us sat, sang, joined arms with dozens of others, were dragged, hauled, thrown into wagons, and I discovered all at once that I had been arrested for civil disobedience for the first time in my life.

Thirty-seven others were arrested with us. The

demonstration had been organized by SNCC. So far as I could see, no one had participated in the sit-in without full knowledge of what was at stake and nobody had joined in without understanding the legal danger. No violence had occurred and there was no roughness from the demonstrators. The only roughness came from the police. Young college students were dragged into a police station and a number were thrown down on the hard concrete so that their heads cracked audibly against the floor. All were allowed bail but court hearing was for Monday. This meant I would have to miss a day of school. I did not like missing school but I hadn't a doubt in my mind but that one day out of school to confirm to myself that I could do something in which I believed would make me a better, not worse, teacher, so the only things I regretted were the lost lessons of that one day. The judge on Monday, confronted by a battery of lawyers who had come forward to defend us without pay, decided at length to throw out the case, only not before recommending to the young people involved in the sit-in that they would do better to go out and picket an employment agency. I would like to have had a chance to answer him.

Next day at school I was not surprised to find some repercussions. The Principal called me in and said that the Deputy Superintendent, Miss Sullivan, had noticed my name in the paper among those hauled into court and had wondered whether I felt I was fulfilling my obligation to the children by spending a day outside of school. I said I had not expected to be arrested but that I knew I would be penalized by the loss of a day's pay and that I did not expect to be arrested again that year. What I didn't add was that I felt I had fulfilled my obligation to these children very well by doing what I did and much better than she. A boy in the schoolyard whom I had taught the summer before and whose mother was the maid of the Reading Teacher took me aside and asked me confidentially if it was true that I had been arrested. He said he had heard I was, but that the Reading Teacher had told his mother "it was nothing." I didn't like her covering up for me that way and so I told him she was wrong. "It was not nothing. It was something. It was something I cared about and something you'll care about too later on." The Reading Teacher only told me that she regretted "the whole thing."

What I regretted most was that Stephen had gotten into trouble the day I was out and he had been punished more roughly than he had ever been punished while I was at school. What happened was that in my absence, one of the other male teachers had come up to cover for me. While he was there Stephen said "God damn you!" to him. He said, "What did you say?" and the little boy said the same thing, "God damn you!" only a little louder than before. The teacher who had to handle this was a good-natured casual person and he told me later that he understood perfectly why Stephen was confused by the rearrangement and that he was not personally bothered and could not have cared less. But the Reading Teacher overheard it and she took Stephen to the Principal's office. The Principal suspended him from the building for five days.

Next morning, when I was back, Stephen suddenly appeared in the doorway of the auditorium, not having the courage to come in, holding his little lunch bag in his hand and looking up out of his pleading hopeful eyes. When he saw me at the blackboard he caught my eye and smiled. He was, however, instantly driven out of the forbidden classroom once again by the Reading Teacher and, a little while later, out of the school building as well. People thought it was extraordinary, funny, unexpected, that such a rotten kid would want so much to come back to school after he had been kicked out. It *was* extraordinary, too, although it was not funny, because he got so little here and the school had done him so much harm. And still he wanted to come in, not knowing what else to do and having perhaps no other place to go. After that morning, and in fact for the duration of five days, the Reading Teacher would pop in on me at nine o'clock and, if Stephen had not yet appeared, she would smile and she would say, "Let's cross our fingers." Then, when he showed up finally, down-regarding and timid, she would say to me glumly: "Do you see what I see standing in the door?"

On a day soon after that I wrote myself a note about Stephen. The note says he did not do his homework for the Math Teacher and was consequently not allowed to receive help in arithmetic from me. It also says that he pleaded with me privately to come over to his house after school to help him with division so that he would have a chance to catch up with the rest of the class. I remember that I felt my willingness rise, and then fall, and then I told him I could not.

In the basement the same day there was a conversation about the Fourth Graders.

"Just a bad group," said one of the teachers. "No one would have stayed."

Another teacher told me: "They got what they deserved. They had those nice older women for teachers and they talked back to them and wouldn't listen to them and so it's their own damn fault they didn't learn."

When we came out of that room there was a Negro mother talking to one of the other teachers by the door. The teacher I had just been talking to muttered to me nervously that he hoped she hadn't heard us . . .

At a teachers' meeting around that time, the Principal gave us some advice that seemed keyed to the same point and that recognized, by implication, some of the unrest and some of the controversy which had been taking place around us. "Please," she said, "be extremely careful in what you say and realize that anything you say may be overheard. People also may repeat your words. I know that none of you would have to be ashamed of anything you say but just remember that anything you say can be twisted and misunderstood." Her use of the word "misunderstood" seemed backwards: I felt she meant the opposite. I received the same impression on another occasion when she came in to talk to me about something else and noticed a little black and white equal pin that I was wearing.

"It's a nice pin," she said to me instantly, "but don't wear it here."

I said to her: "All it means is equal."

She answered immediately, always confident, never without authority: "I know it. And that's fine. But you never know when it could be misunderstood."

I thought that astonishing. "How could it be misunderstood? Look at it. All it is is an equal sign. Who could misunderstand it?"

She answered me: "You never can tell."

I asked her if she meant my supervisor from the School Department. Was he the one who might not understand? I said: "Do you think he's going to think it's for a fund drive?"

She laughed at that and told me: "Oh come now! We're not as unsophisticated as that!"

I did not answer her but I felt that she was very unsophisticated to think that I could have believed what she had told me.

Other changes came into our school during that period—some of them due to the arrival of a new Negro teacher. There already were a small number of Negro teachers in the school, but in this case there was a great difference because the new teacher was from a different background and had had a different kind of education than any of the others.

He was a great deal more sophisticated than almost all of the other Negro teachers, yet he was not for that reason any more willing to go along with gestures of white tokenism but was, on the contrary, far more shrewd and bitter and percipient and cool. I remember the day on which he came into the school because it was on the same morning that two of the first American astronauts were shot up into space. It was not long after James Reeb's death in Selma. Nobody at school had thought of a school program to discuss Alabama and its significance for us, but the decision had been made to bring everyone up into the auditorium to look at the space flight on television. Two giant sets were propped up on the stage and the pupils were prepared for the program by the Assistant Principal. Then, with some fascination and some boredom, they watched and listened to all the curious language about everything being "Go" and all systems being "A-okay" and the flight being a real honey and so forth, the whole rest of the Buck Rogers-Jack Armstrong lingo that surrounds the public relations aspect of a serious event. While all this was happening, the new teacher stood a few feet from me and, when I said to him, "What do you think of it?" he said: "I think it's boring." And then he added: "I think that the whole business is absurd." I didn't think it was absurd, not scientifically anyway, and I am sure that, if he had been questioned, he would have admitted also that the space-shot must have technical importance. But what he meant became clear right after that when he said: "There are more important things going on in this room and in this country and not one hundred miles above the surface of the earth."

Afterward I told the Reading Teacher that I thought he was going to create some differences in the school, and that proved to be correct. He was appointed, I believe, a provisional teacher, like myself, only instead of having a class to teach upstairs he had

been put in the basement to work as an assistant to
an older teacher. The man to whom he was assigned was not well qualified. He was, I thought,
one of the least competent teachers in the school.
His attitude toward the children varied between dislike and apathy—with apathy, of a sleepy, sluggish,
heavy-footed nature, being the overriding feeling.
When I had asked him once about the curriculum
he was teaching, he answered me, pleasantly: "I
figure I give them the same curriculum that they'd
be getting any place else. If I put in a little less
meat, I figure that they get the same number of po-
tatoes." He talked a lot about killing crabgrass on
his lawn and about the change in the neighborhood
we taught in and he kept his class of forty pupils
well in line by a hefty use of the rattan. I used to
think that, within a dreary school and in an awful
cellar room with such an overload of pupils, for a
man of very few qualifications he probably did a
reasonably good job. But the arrival of the new
Negro teacher suddenly changed things.

The change was brought about because, by all
obvious credentials, the new Negro teacher was
so many miles out of the older teacher's league.
Educated at Michigan State, cultivated, thoroughly
resourceful, the new teacher literally could not open
his mouth without shattering the regular teacher
with insecurity. The other thing, of course, which
was most important, was that the boys in the room,
kept down all year by the old potato-teacher, re-
sponded promptly to the obvious differences between
the two men who were now in front of them each
morning and got a rapid-fire education, and what
must have appeared to them as a carefully planned
indoctrination, in the natural advantages of being
black. Almost everything the regular teacher could
do, it seemed, the new teacher could do better.
The only serious problem, as the new teacher quickly
told me, was that he was getting almost no oppor-

tunity to teach. Sometimes he got to do a little history, sometimes a little bit of something else. If the carpentry shop was not occupied, he could take a group of boys in there for remedial work in math or reading. They would have to sit between drills and jigsaws or whatever other equipment might be around them or else on top of sawdust-covered planks, but at least it did give him a little chance to teach. When that room was occupied, he would take the boys up into our auditorium but, perhaps because he had a higher sense of his own dignity than other teachers had—or else perhaps a higher sense of dignity of the Negro boys—he refused finally to work there, saying flatly that to work with his pupils in such a crossfire of voice was futile. The futility of which he spoke was the futility amidst which I had been working, without much objection, all that year.

His open clean objections were uncluttered by the fear that tied down certain other Negro teachers, of losing their jobs or losing the chance for the small good they could get done with their one class, because he was looking toward a much larger goal and had, it seemed, a much less provincial and much less parochial past. He also had very few of the white inhibitions that had rendered me for so long rather ineffective, for the very uncomplicated reason that his skin was black. Yet many of our ideas, independently arrived at, proved to be the same and we soon grew to be friends.

I went over to his house one Saturday and met his wife and daughter and talked with him about what was happening in the school and in the neighborhood and we developed the idea of joining in a meeting with local parents and offering them some information about what was going on. Although I felt a knot of instantaneous fear in my stomach at the thought of what I was doing, I knew I couldn't back out and I knew while we were talking that I was going to be obliged to do it. The other teacher, whom I will call Carl, contacted some of the parents and the result of his telephoning, which followed a few days later, was perhaps one of the first real parents' and teachers' meetings ever held in a Negro neighborhood of Boston because it was not under the supervision of the school administration and it was therefore honest and untrammeled by any false supplications to the power of the school. The meeting was held at a church near the school building. It was not large but it brought about half a dozen teachers from various Boston schools and about fifteen or twenty parents from our school. The new teacher spoke first and then I did and then we answered questions and we told the parents, in answer to their inquiries, about the classes in the cellar, those in the auditorium, the outdated curriculum, the dilapidated materials and outdated textbooks and the overall worthlessness of the compensatory program as a viable means of making up for the deficiencies of a segregated school. A mother of Fifth Grade children was surprised to be told of a practice by which an entire class would be rattanned for the misbehavior of one pupil. A Fourth Grade mother was embittered to learn for the first time that one of the Fourth Grades had been stuck all year with a teacher who could not control children and who had already had similar difficulties within another school. Other parents had not been advised by the Principal that reading levels were far behind the national average at our school and that the reading levels seemed to be growing worse with every year the children spent in school.

The outcome of this meeting was a decision on the part of the parents to make a complaint to the school in the form of stated demands and also to join in a picket at School Committee Headquarters which had been begun by a Boston minister and then had been joined and supported by members of various parent organizations. As soon as possible after that meeting, both Carl and I went in and told the Principal about it. We did not want to leave the chance that she might view it as something secret or something of which we were ashamed. It is true that, when I went in to talk to her, my hands were shaking and my voice was trembling badly. At a distance from the school I had joined in protests without reluctance but here it seemed different and it created a great deal of anxiety in me when the confrontation of opposites came so close. I did not tell her about our meeting truculently, but quietly. I said it was something I believed in and that nothing said at the meeting would have been news to her, but I added that I knew very well it was still the kind of meeting of which she would have to strongly disapprove.

And that was so. She said it had been a mistake. She told me also that she did not know if a person accepting the pay of the Boston School Committee had the right to join in a picket against his own employer, adding that she felt it was an improper way to do things and that in time many problems with which she and I were both concerned would undoubtedly begin to be corrected, although not due to pressure from people who were misinformed. I just said quietly that I felt she was wrong, that I was not misinformed, nor were the parents any longer. So I went out of her office feeling more free and more at peace with myself than I had felt the whole year long, and taught, I imagine, more effectively for it too, although the Reading Teacher told me later that, since I had gone in to talk to her, the Principal had been in a very unpleasant state of mind.

Carl, as it happened, left our school almost as suddenly as he had come there. Four or five weeks of it was about all that he could stand and then one day he just walked out. The teacher who had worked with him downstairs said of him, "He couldn't take it," meaning, I guess, that the children were too rough for him, but this was not the case. And upstairs the Reading Teacher told me: "It just doesn't look good for them. Even if he did feel it was degrading to him here. He had no right to walk out on his own people. The other Negro teachers are embarrassed." But I thought that Carl had a clearer sense of what was happening in this building than some of the more traditional Negro teachers had. And so, even though I would not have said it to them since I had no wish to act as a judge of them and of what they had to endure, still in one way, not as a teacher but just as a person, I admired him more than I admired any of the rest: because he had the courage not only of his convictions but also of his race. Selfishly, for the sake of having a friend I could talk to openly, I found I wished that he had stayed.

THIRTEEN

FOR a number of months the State Board of Education had been preparing a full report on racial imbalance in Massachusetts schools. At last, one day in April, the report was released. It was not an accusatory or unforgiving piece of writing and it was in fact rather moderate and conciliatory in its tone. But its meaning was clear and its content was strong and its recommendations were straightforward and specific. As a piece of writing, it represented in a sense the conscience of that part of our community which thinks and cares and lives by principle but which apparently cannot affect the outcome of a vote. The report dominated much of the news media for several days. Signatures presented in approval of the report included again those of Ralph Lowell, Lewis Weinstein, Erwin Canham and Cardinal Cushing. The report was 132 pages long. On page two appeared these summarizing words:

> Our conclusions are clear. Racial imbalance represents a serious conflict with the American creed of equal opportunity. It is detrimental to sound education in the following ways: It does serious educational damage to Negro children by impairing their confidence, distorting their self-image, and lowering their motivation. It does moral damage by encouraging prejudice within children regardless of their color. It represents an inaccurate picture of life to both white and Negro children and prepares them inadequately for a multi-racial community, nation, and world. It too often pro-

duces inferior educational facilities in the predominantly Negro schools. It squanders valuable human resources by impairing the opportunities of many Negro children to prepare for the professional and vocational requirements of our technological society. It is imperative that we begin to end this harmful system of separation. The means are at hand. Each day of delay is a day of damage to the children of our Commonwealth.

The report then summarized the damage exclusively to Negro children in these words:

Educators and social scientists have produced a large body of evidence documenting the conclusion that racial separation has powerful and injurious impact on the self-image, confidence, motivation, and the school achievement of Negro children. It is not difficult to understand why racial separation is harmful to Negro children. Outside of the school the Negro child and his family too often have heard the message, "Keep out, stay back, you are not wanted." He and his family have too often been made to feel different and inferior. The racially imbalanced school reinforces that feeling. Inside the school, the young faces are almost all black. The older faces—those of the teachers, the ones in charge—are mostly white. Does the child wonder why only black children go to this school? A child cannot comprehend the subtle difference between illegal segregation in the South and racial imbalance in the North. He sees only that he is Negro and almost all his schoolmates are Negroes. The separation of some children "from others of similar age and qualification because of their race generates a feeling of inferiority as to their status that may affect their hearts and minds in a way unlikely ever to be undone."

Recommended for closing as soon after 1965 as possible was a list of a number of the most highly segregated and most dilapidated public schools in Boston. Among these was the school in which I taught.

Immediately upon the report's release, the various members of the School Committee began putting forth defensive statements. Mr. Lee, whose reactions were reported in detail by the Boston papers, seemed unmoved by the State Board's emphasis and eloquence and concerned only that the authors of the report had forgotten to give the Negro child the "special instruction he needs, in his own neighborhood school." Lee defended to the hilt the nature of the present set-up. "It seems to me," he said, "the pupil from the unprosperous Negro family is usually backward in school, otherwise there wouldn't be any concern or any state commission report for the overcoming of his backwardness." He maintained as well that "white children do not want to be transported into schools with a large proportion of backward pupils from unprospering Negro families who will slow down their education . . . White children do not want large numbers of backward pupils from unprospering Negro families shipped into their present mainly white schools, either."

Mrs. Hicks was equally prompt in coming to the defense of the present set-up, but she concerned herself with somewhat different aspects of the report. Focusing on some of the fiscal and transportational suggestions made by the State commission, she derided them as unworkable and undemocratic and protested, furthermore, "What they are trying to do is set up a dictatorship." Civil rights representatives were bewildered and enraged a few days later when they asked the School Committee to discuss the report with them on an open basis and the School Committee chairman was obliged to confess that she could not do this until she had had a chance to read it. What became apparent to observers was that Mrs. Hicks did not mind speaking of the report if it would bring her press attention, but that she had no serious intention of ever dealing with it.

Throughout this time, naturally, there was a vast amount of public controversy and a television sta-

tion in Boston apparently decided it would be an
effective part of news coverage to come to visit in
one of the segregated schools. The one they picked
was the school where I was working and the consequence of this was that we lost about half a day
of teaching while the School Department sent in a
crew of repairmen to try to make the school look a
little less dilapidated before the television cameras
got there. My own classes were interrupted, as were
those of several other teachers, and the morning was
lost for most of the children while repairmen tore
out windows and put in new glass-panes, sometimes
only a few feet from the children's desks. That evening, we had a chance to see our Principal on television as she replied to the news reporter that there
was nothing inferior, so far as she could tell, about a
racially imbalanced school, that there was no damage, so far as she could see, to Negro children, that
there was no disadvantage in this kind of schooling—
at least, not at this level and not at this age—and not
at least as far as she could tell. I wondered if the
television station knew what a hoax had been perpetrated upon it and whether the reporter and the
photographer would have been surprised to know
that it took their visit to our school building before
our class could have new windows.

The major point behind all of this, of course,
is the extraordinary bravado with which the School
Committee waved off criticism and rejected out of
hand a report that had been signed by so many distinguished citizens. More extraordinary, still, was the
fact that the people of Boston, at least the ones who
were most vocal, seemed to back up the School Committee and Mrs. Hicks in person to the hilt. Watching events at that time, and talking with various
people in the city, was for me a disheartening education in the nature of the attitudes of American people, and it caused me to wonder, as I have been
obliged to wonder since, whether there is any longer
a real connection between the preferences and cruel-

ties of American citizens and the kinds of assertions about fair play and freedom that we are attempting to sell to other nations. The worst of it was that so much of the cruelty could be expressed in the guise of paternalism and so many of the staunchest bigots in the city could convince themselves that they were acting and speaking out of decent feelings.

I remember a talk that I had around that time with a man who owned a lot of property in the Negro section and who made a great deal of money out of this property, but still retained a very special image of the Negro people whose rents comprised his livelihood. He was a good-natured man in his late fifties and we were riding in his car. As we drove through the ghetto, I remember that he gestured around him and said to me confidently that it was not the fault of the Negroes, they just didn't have the background or preparation to know how to live. The problem, he said, was not due to them but due to the poor education they were getting. Encouraged by this second statement—because he seemed so blunt and honest—I asked him if he thought then that the problem was that the schools were not doing as well as they should. But now suddenly, as soon as I put it that way, he reversed himself completely and he took an opposite position: "No sir, I don't," he told me right away. "The schools are doing a wonderful job with what they've got. You take these kids from homes like those and parents from all over no place and everything all mixed up and nobody living right and how on earth do you expect a day in school to change that child's life?" So I told him then about our school, saying in particular that we had two classes which did not even have their own rooms, others in which there were many disturbed or retarded children, two classrooms in a cellar, others with broken windows, rooms with windows that did not open, and several other things like that. His answer had two parts:

One answer was that "we did it, and we never had

any fancy schools either and nothing special for us, no special classes or stuff like that. And if we did it then I don't see why can't they?" And the other argument was: "Why out in the country they walk miles to school and they all sit in one big classroom, farmers' children all of them, and they are good American kids and do their lessons and you don't hear anybody saying that those kids don't get an education because they do get one and they get a damn fine one and so do these kids right here in Boston if they would only pull themselves up and do something for themselves for a change and if their mothers and fathers, when they even have them, would just stop living off the government and would straighten their own lives out too."

I said: "Then you feel the schools are really doing pretty well?"

And he said to me: "Darn right. I think Mrs. Hicks in there is terrific and she's doing a wonderful fine job. Honestly," he said finally, "if you could see the way some of the parents around here bring up those kids, your heart would go out to them—to the little ones—the way they make them lie and sneak."

These comments from this landlord, an educated man who went on regular trips to Europe and had placed his own child in a sophisticated little French school outside of Boston, must be repeated by thousands of people in our city every year. Certainly they were consonant with the views expressed by a great many Bostonians during the days after the State Report came out. I remember that the radio stations were deluged all day long with calls from people who wanted to say on the air how they felt about the problem. An alarmingly large number of them, so far as I could tell, were on the School Committee's side. Call after call came in from people of our city who said in essence: "We don't go for all those trouble-makers" and "We're all with you, Mrs. Hicks!" The *Globe* reported that she was

personally swamped with letters of congratulation.
"LETTERS OF SUPPORT POUR IN ON MRS. HICKS" was
the headline of one week later. The letters focused
on one of many recommendations of the report, but
a recommendation which quickly became the heart of
the whole matter. This was a recommendation that,
for immediate relief of the imbalance problem, a program of two-way bussing should be instituted for
several thousand children between predominantly
white and predominantly Negro schools. This
brought Mrs. Hicks her largest piles of mail:

Sacks of mail, bundles of telegrams and countless
telephone calls supporting her stand against the
bussing of children outside their home districts
were reported today by School Committee chairman Mrs. Louise Day Hicks. The volume of cor-
respondence is such that Mrs. Hicks said she hired
three girls to handle it for her . . . The communi-
cations have come from people in every walk of
life, according to the school board chairman. Parents, clergymen and public officials everywhere appear to be opposed to bussing school children . . .
Mrs. Hicks said. One admirer of Mrs. Hicks sent
her an azalea plant bearing a card which read,
"Hicksey, you're wonderful." A Roxbury woman
wrote in a letter, "Keep up the good work, our
Mrs. Hicks." From Florence, Mass., came a communication saying, "Three percent of the population of the state is making the other 97 percent
sit up and do tricks. It's really refreshing to have
a public official like you to say exactly what most
people are thinking. You are fighting a good fight."
From Worcester came a letter advising Mrs. Hicks,
"There are many people like you who are opposed
to rabble-rousing." From a Newton mother came a
wire simply saying, "Congratulations to one woman
with some backbone." From a Baptist pastor in
a north of Boston community came a terse tele-
gram saying, "You are right." Only a handful of
the thousands of letters, wires and phone calls expressed opposition to Mrs. Hicks' position, she said.

The statements quoted above were for the most part not coarse or vulgar, but just loaded with bigotry. The people who used the coarser terms, however, sometimes got quoted in the newspaper also, and during the same period there were several withering quotations of the latter sort appearing in the Boston press. There had been, for example, not long before, the annual St. Patrick's Day parade, a major event in a heavily Irish Catholic city, and this year again—just like the year before—a handful of the people who keep Mrs. Hicks in power gave up all pretences of tolerance or Christian kindliness and let themselves loose for one regular old-fashioned American session of drunkenness and bigotry.

"Trouble," reported the *Globe*, "cropped up at I Street, where a group of youths in their twenties held forth, their beer mugs held high. One stepped out from the gutter and spewed a mouthful of beer on Archie E. Dickerson, a Negro, from Roxbury . . . The parade hadn't gone a block when another youth staggered out and cursed a priest . . . At Perkins Square, Father Serino flew out of the line of march for a second time when a young group in front of a bar chanted, 'Nigger lovin b————. Never mind the niggers, join the army. You holy niggers.'"

About a month later, Gilbert Caldwell, a minister and one of the most respected leaders of the 65,000 Negro people of Boston, went out to the neighborhood of Hyde Park to attend a meeting on fair housing. At the time that he was there he got up bravely and spoke out after several individuals who were members of the audience began asking questions and making statements that had an apparent anti-Negro edge. The Boston *Globe* of April 19 reported this: "Mr. Caldwell commented that he detected the same hatred in the speakers which would get him clubbed down in Selma . . . After his statement one of these racists rose and shouted that he would never club down a Negro in Boston—he would spit on him."

It was during the same period of racial unrest and surfacing bigotry that we had a memorable teachers' meeting at my school. At the meeting the Principal recounted to us the statistical facts about the unplaced special students in our classes. She said she was afraid that she was going to be able to find space in special class for, at best, only eight out of forty-two during the academic year ahead. For the rest she had to admit that she could promise nothing. She did not say why, did not discuss the fact that we did not even have an extra room in which to teach them, and did not point out that perhaps fifteen or twenty thousand dollars and a willingness to bus the children or to re-district the whole area might have begun to solve the problem if the School Superintendent or School Committee had been willing. These people, of course, were not willing and one of the reasons for this, along with many others, was that they had some other and more immediate uses for these funds. What uses the School Committee did have for that money became clarified in a series of items that appeared in the press at around the same time.

As I read it in the *Globe*, the School Committee voted, first, to add a total of six new high-paying positions to the top of an already top-heavy school system administration in the form of six new "district superintendents" at salaries of $17,000 per year. In a year and a season in which desks could not be found for students to work at in view of their teachers and in which money could not be found to paint walls, put lights in basements, or replace cardboard windows with glass panes, it seemed the height of political effrontery to create six new posts costing a total of $102,000 a year for people who would not even be in the schools but who would be sitting in office chairs up some place at the top. What about twelve new genuinely qualified teachers to begin to educate Edward and the hundreds of other unplaced special students in the city? What about one hundred thousand dollars' worth of integrated readers, of modern histories and geography texts, of tape recorders, record players, poetry recordings, movies, slides and prints? Why six new officials with six new fat and heavy salaries? Were they needed? Or was the need a dire one? Would lives have been lost without them? What about hiring ten good teachers, a qualified counselor and a full-time psychiatrist for the discipline school at which I had worked? What about the boys there? What about the children with twenty-five substitute teachers at William Lloyd Garrison? What about some school libraries? What about some bright cans of pink, green, blue, and light yellow paint to cheer up our gloomy walls?

If this one act was not enough, the School Committee also voted at this time to give a salary increment to some of the old administrators who were already at the top. These latter boosts included a jump of Mr. Ohrenberger's salary from an already high $26,000 to $30,000, a jump of Miss Sullivan's salary from $19,000 to $23,000, and similar jumps in pay for several other people. Reaction to this pay-boost was considerable and even the Mayor of Boston had something angry to say. The *Globe* reported his comments in a story that appeared on its front page:

Mayor Collins today angrily accused the Boston School Committee of being "extraordinarily open-handed with tax-payers' money." Commenting on $4000 pay hikes granted last week to top echelon school administrators, Collins fumed: "I am appalled by what I see here. It is difficult to see how any member of the School Committee can be so lavish with public funds. I always thought," continued the mayor, "that elected representatives were responsible to all citizens of Boston, all taxpayers and also to those with children who go to our schools." [The *Globe* continued:] These salary increases for the top executives came as a surprise to city officials because salaries of the top school officials had been raised $1000 less than two years ago.

A few days later, the *Globe* also reported this:

The $4000 hike was the straw that broke the camel's back as far as the mayor was concerned. It would mean that . . . Ohrenberger would go . . . to $30,000; business manager Leo J. Burke and Deputy Superintendent Marguerite Sullivan . . . to $23,000, and the six assistant superintendents who recommended the raises . . . to $21,000. All would earn more than the mayor under these schedules. Mrs. Louise Day Hicks, School Committee chairman . . . said she thought the school budget had been properly balanced before being sent to the mayor. Asked what she meant by "balanced," Mrs. Hicks said that money was taken out of other accounts to take care of the raises. She pointed out that $1 million was taken from the alterations and repairs account. She said further that the committee deducted from "our budget certain items for educational expansion programs in order to give the raises."

The connection could not have been made more clear: Four thousand more for Mr. Ohrenberger. Four thousand more for Miss Sullivan. Thirty thousand more in all for these already well-paid administrators, and just that much less for alterations and repair and educational improvement. I thought that this was a remarkable self-indictment on the part of those who ran the schools. The result of all of this in practical terms, as it filtered down through talk and gossip within the school itself, was that most expansion projects which had been planned for the compensatory program would now have to be curtailed, that repairs to buildings would stay at a minimum, and that very little would be done during the immediate year to improve the quality of textbooks in our school. All of this was directly connected to the fact that Superintendent Ohrenberger, along with the rest of his top staff, had agreed to be rewarded with a substantial and unneeded boost in pay from a salary which was already a great deal higher than he could have earned in almost any other sort of educational employment with the kind of qualifications that he had.

The animosity in the Negro community against the School Committee chairman, as a consequence of this action and others, became very great. It did not surprise me to find the following item on the front page of the *Globe* about eight weeks later:

MRS. HICKS GETS GUN PERMIT FOR PROTECTION

Boston School Committee Chairman Mrs. Louise Day Hicks has obtained a permit to carry a gun to protect "her life and property." The authorization was granted to Mrs. Hicks May 20 at Boston Police Headquarters . . . According to police records, the School Committee chairman gave no instances why she felt compelled to take out the permit other than the "protection of life and property." With this permit, Mrs. Hicks can purchase a weapon and carry it anywhere inside the Bay State. As a result of her stand on the question of alleged de facto segregation in Boston, Mrs. Hicks has been constantly harassed by telephone calls and visits to her home . . . More recently Boston police have been forced to clear a path through Civil Rights pickets for Mrs. Hicks following meetings at the Boston School Committee . . . Mrs. Hicks has praised the police for their efforts in her behalf.

I thought it was unfortunate if people had threatened Mrs. Hicks, but it could not be news to anyone that she had made herself the object of a great deal of hate. The sense of outrage felt about the salary hikes, about her stand on segregation, about her unwillingness even to talk seriously about the State Board's scrupulous report, created a groundswell of seething discontent that could be felt in every Negro neighborhood of town. During the course of six weeks, two of the most highly segregated schools in Roxbury were burned and one of them was gutted badly. At my own school unknown per-

sons, possibly students, entered the building on weekends to empty desks, slash curtains, scatter records,
scratch obscenities on already obscenely dirty walls.
The curtains in our auditorium, already torn and
filthy and ugly, were stabbed and slashed dozens of
times by an unknown person during a break that
took place in late May. Whoever had been in the
school had also upset a drawer from my own desk,
and scattered papers around, although they did not
take money that was in partial view.

After the first of the two fires that I have referred
to, Mrs. Hicks appeared, surrounded by reporters,
to view the ruins. She was quoted by the Boston
Herald as noting a "strange coincidence" in the close
proximity of time between this act of vandalism
and the recent civil rights march that had accom-
panied a visit to Boston by Martin Luther King.
This sounded to me like an idea I'd heard before.
It seemed to me to be the same thing that teachers
in Boston were implying when they said that, in the
old days, the Negroes took what they were given
without complaining, whereas now, with the advent
of civil rights commotion and rabble-rousing, everybody was bitter and angry and the children all were
getting up in arms. Mrs. Hicks' statement also
sounded similar to the statements of certain racist
leaders in the Deep South who would blame the
troubles that come upon them not upon their own
active sins, or sins of omission, but rather upon the
interlopers, civil rights leaders and troublemakers
who move in, as they would put it, "from the outside" to get the people angry and to stir the people
up. So now Mrs. Hicks connected the arson of this
public school to a Nobel Prize winner's visit. But all
that surprised me was that every one of those schools
had not been burned down yet by an outraged population when so many of them were obvious firetraps
and when every one of them bred so much igniting
hate.

FOURTEEN

THERE are, I suppose, all kinds of prejudice and discrimination, and not all of it is either obvious or overtly brutal. There is also a kind of prejudice that is swaddled around with appearances of benevolence and of compassion and the kind that is expressed commonly not as an explicit hostility to Negroes so much as an affectionate preference for a "different type of child." The teachers at my school who revealed this kind of feeling most consistently tended to be among the older women—and among these were the Reading Teacher and Art Teacher. The Reading Teacher expressed it mainly as a favoritism for the children who were most obedient and successful by her standards, or whose parents were most like herself and hence people with whom she could chat most comfortably. The favoritism of the Art Teacher, in some ways very much like her, was in one respect more selective and more specific. For she was involved not only with the children who were most like her, and whose parents were most familiar to her, but she was also and more particularly bound up with children who were Jewish.

There was an incident illustrative of this feeling, which had to do with a very unusual and very appealing white child in my class. This was a girl named Susan who had impressed me not only for her exceptional academic work but also for her marked and affectionate friendliness to Stephen. On a number of days, in a great many hours when he must have been very near the bottom of despair,

I had seen her go over to him, where he sat in the
row next to her, and offer in a friendly way to help
him with his work. On a number of mornings she
had sat and done arithmetic with him for forty or
fifty minutes or an hour, and I felt grateful to her,
and even more fond of her, for her uninhibited
kindness. This girl happened to be Jewish.

One day in the spring, the mother of that child
came up to school to tell us they were moving.
Having ascertained that both the Art Teacher and
I were Jewish, she caught us together on the stairway and she told us both familiarly and, somehow,
knowingly and intimately, that her daughter would
finish off this year but would not be back again
in September. Without hesitation she looked up at
us both in a manner of private understanding,
nodded as before a wave of indefinable but ugly nature, and explained to us flatly that her daughter was
growing up and that she simply did not want her to
be where there were "so many colored." I do not
know whether or not it was obvious to her how I
reacted to this. But there was no question at all about
how the Art Teacher reacted. She told the mother
instantly that she was naturally going to miss her
daughter greatly, because she was a talented and
hard-working child, but she also made it clear that
she thought that this was a very wise decision. We
talked about it together later on when the mother
was not present. When I expressed my disappointment, the Art Teacher looked up at me with curiosity
and she said to me, openly enough:

"Who has she got to play with?"

I rattled off the names of a half dozen girls in
my class with whom she not only could play, but
did play, and apparently without bad consequences.
The Art Teacher smiled at this, however, and immediately asserted to me flatly that "none of them,"
meaning the Negro children, "are her kind." An instant later, she added: "Maybe one of the chil-

dren . . ." But that one turned out to be a child who had served her frequently as a kind of token person, a little girl whose name she brought forward to me occasionally, at times when it was necessary, in order to assure me that she could express fondness for a Negro child also.

I asked her if she did not care that, after Susan and her mother and father and sisters moved away, this was going to be only that much more of a ghetto and one of the kindest and most valuable of the white children would be gone.

The Art Teacher didn't worry over what I had said so much as she "speculated" upon it, fingered it as it were, considering its inadequacies, and then came to the pre-determined decision that I was wrong: "What is there for them among people like these? It is the right of every family to want to live among its own kind." She said: "It is important for you to think of it not as moving away from Negroes but just as wanting to be among Jews. They are Jews and it is their right to have a synagogue and Jewish friends nearby."

I said: "She told us colored. She said it is because there are so many colored in this part."

The Art Teacher shut it out and just denied it. "It is not," she said, "moving away from Negro people. It is just wanting to live where there are more Jews."

This view may perhaps seem both innocent and natural to many people. It is a way of disguising the real issue which the Art Teacher shared with the vast majority of white people, including of course a great many Jewish people, in America. But the same attitude, expressed as nostalgia and emotional preference on the one hand, could flash out suddenly in an instant of hypocrisy or of stark cruelty on the other. The cruelty was seen, for example, in the manner in which she was able to dismiss Stephen's drawings, tearing them up and designating them as "garbage" because they were not like the drawings of her former pupils, when in fact they were not garbage at all and when, furthermore, they were almost the only thing in the world that Stephen had to hold onto for pride and for encouragement and for any kind of self-esteem. It must have been cataclysmic for him to have sat there and looked up at her in her fury and seen her ripping his drawings across in one sweeping gesture and then dropping them in the wastebasket right in front of everybody's eyes.

The hypocrisy involved in her narrow favoritism was revealed in several ways. One of them was in the case of Frederick, the boy who was whipped and then hospitalized and whose cause she effectively sidestepped and refused to face head-on but to whom she then sent a get-well card while he was convalescing. A different kind of ambiguity appeared in her curious ball-balancing in regard to civil rights. The Art Teacher, like a number of the other schoolteachers in the building, paid a fairly regular and steadfast lip service to a kind of halfway liberalism. She gave an annual contribution, I believe, to the local branch of the NAACP and saw no inconsistency between this and her stated attitudes toward Negro children or her attitude toward Stephen. In school, the end-result of her inconsistencies came down to a specific discrimination in the way that she would deal with pupils, depending on whether they were Negro or Jewish. I found it so obvious that I came out and questioned her about it once. I don't remember how I said it—it was always an agony for me to pose a question like that. "It is true, isn't it, that you feel more easy, more intimate, somehow more committed when you are dealing with the white kids, and can do more for them in an extra way, than when you are dealing with the others?" Something of that sort. I said it perhaps in a way that was even more blurred than that, but the answer was direct and frank and unevasive:

"I am thinking about the Jewish children," she replied to me. "It is this remnant which I cannot help having most at heart. I feel it is my duty to do something for them since Judaism has been central in my career and it is this remnant—and I am also including you—who have always been at the center of my life."

Despite the fact that she included me within her blessing, I did not feel honored but ashamed. When she explained to me that what she was trying to do was not to deny any Negro child but rather only "to save this Jewish remnant," I thought but I didn't say that this was the worst possible way to be Jewish and save Judaism. I thought that a less selective and more open and honest donation of her powers to the children before us who had the most to bear would have been the real way to be greatly Jewish in the tradition of Jewish ethics and morality and in the tradition, as well, of those many hundreds of Jewish students and Jewish leaders who, in recent years, have been in the immediate forefront of the civil rights movement in America in general and right here in Boston in particular. It does not take any longer in Boston than it does in much of the rest of the country to look around and take cognizance of the significant numbers of Jewish people among the citizens who man the anti-discriminatory agencies, who sign the protests and battle in the law courts and join the picket lines. Here, as in New York City, as in the Deep South, as in much of the nation, rabbis and Jewish community leaders have walked side by side with priests and ministers in the cause of Negro freedom. I therefore found it discordant and disappointing to think that this schoolteacher, who spoke so proudly of her Judaism, could hold herself a liberal and consider herself an ethical person and even contribute money so generously to the various Negro causes, yet move through life and through the lives of countless Negro children with an attitude of such soaring discrimination and with an outlook of such overt and such unjustifiable favoritism.

Perhaps I can demonstrate this attitude more clearly if I give one additional example of the way that it revealed itself. The Art Teacher, like a number of older Jewish people, would frequently draw an unfavorable comparison between the kinds of homes the Negro people kept in Roxbury and the homes of the Jews who had lived in these blocks only about ten or fifteen years before. The Art Teacher had often assured me that the Negroes whose children we taught did not know how to keep up property, that the homes in that area had really been beautiful once when the Jewish people lived there, but now had been allowed to go to pieces through lack of proper maintenance and appropriate care. If and when a time came that she visited in a home belonging to Negroes whom she considered above the racial average, still she could not resist the urge, perhaps the need or the compulsion, to differentiate between that home and the kind of home that she felt a Jewish family would have lived in.

I have spoken earlier in this book of a little girl whose mother died in childbirth and whose mother's funeral the teachers who attended it had derided scornfully. Although I was not allowed out of school to go to the funeral, I did get a chance to go over and visit the child and her father in the afternoon. When I came back to school the next morning I happened to mention it to the Art Teacher and, when she asked me what I thought of their home, I said absolutely honestly that I thought that it was a pretty nice home. Her response to that was withering. She smiled at me tolerantly, as if I was too charitable or naive or not perceptive, and she told me with a care in her choice of words and with a curious kind of pained precision: "I wouldn't say that it was a nice home, Johnny, if you know what I mean," and touching the sleeve of my arm or just grazing it rather with a sense of conspiratorial understanding as she said it. "I wouldn't say it was a nice home. I would say that it was a nice *Negro* home. The two things are not the same." I do not know whether the words alone, without the sound of her voice, convey the sweep that seemed implicit in them. The first and most unsettling echo for the sound of a "Negro home," to my own ears, was the "Jewish store" and "Jewish money" and "Jewish press" of Nazi writings. Did the Art Teacher not see the bitterness of what she, as an ardent Jewish chauvinist, was stating? This upset me deeply. I felt later that it was one of the roughest expressions of a gross and conscious and intentional class-condescension that I had ever heard.

Despite my general silence and hesitation, I must have shown enough of my reaction at certain times to make her wonder. For every so often, after that, the Art Teacher would come forward and, with very little prior conversation, perhaps no more than a casual word or two, she would just bluntly say something to me about her feelings which was obviously intended to be in her defense.

"It's chauvinism," she would say to me all of a sudden, and when she said it she would smile or laugh as if it were a harmless, humorous idea. "It's chauvinism, not prejudice," she'd tell me. And she seemed to gain some kind of reassurance or satisfaction out of saying it so often, as if the more times she was able to say it the more it might be true.

"Honestly, when Joey acts up, I feel terrible. I feel worse. I feel ashamed. Because he's Jewish. I don't see any merit in Stephen. I think he is a contemptible mean child. When Joey acts up it is a different feeling. He is a child I want to save."

I don't think she could have realized how unjust she sounded when she said this. Day after day she would return to it, explaining to me the difference in her mind between discriminating against Negroes (a bad thing) and favoring Jews (okay). She would hold up before my pupils the artwork of a previous white and Jewish generation and would say to them, with only a flash of hesitation: "These are the kinds of pictures that the children who came to this school used to do here. You children couldn't do it." There was a holding-back sometimes on the last part, and perhaps those final words were rarely spoken. But the implication was so clear, and the facts so wrong. For there were children in the classes she taught with talent she would never even discover for imaginative work of a sort of which, possibly, she could never even conceive. I found this reminiscent of my conversation with the Reading Teacher. After I had asked her insistently a dozen times whether Angelina did not have talent, then she would start conceding to me sometimes that Angelina actually could draw. But when I had suggested an unusual summer program over in Cambridge as opposed to the Museum School for this pupil, she had assured me that the Museum School was good enough for a child like Angelina.

At first in the school I did not have any stronger opinion about that kind of attitude than to think that some of those women could be incredibly tough on kids who disagreed with them or who would not serve as mirrors for their personalities. I just thought they were too quick and positive and too eager to hold onto the accomplishments of other generations. Now I think it was more than that, for they did not really believe that children could have ideas that they themselves did not have or talents and tastes with which they were not familiar. They did not believe that children—white or Negro, Irish or Jewish—could be people different from what they thought children ought to be, and still be admirable, still worth teaching, still worth respecting, still perhaps worth listening to and even learning from. I do not think that any of those three teachers ever did a great deal of listening. They listened for right answers, perhaps, but that was different, because then they were only listening for what they had already decided to be true. In one respect, this manner they had, this way of looking only for their own reflection, was more offensive and more troubling than the simple race-hatred of some of the other kinds of teachers. I am sure neither has a place in a good school system, but the latter has the advantage of being honest.

FIFTEEN

A YOUNG teacher without powerful connections or impressive affiliations does not last long in the Boston school system unless he learns to remain relatively silent about the things that he sees. It is a different story with a teacher who is simply incompetent. Teachers who are senile, physically degenerate, mentally unstable, have been kept on often for months, in some cases for years, before the school system has begun to address itself effectively to the question of whether or not they were really teaching anything. This was the situation with the Fourth Grade teacher in my school, neither senile nor degenerate, but certainly unstable to the point of being a considerable threat to the mental health and education of a class of children. Beginning in the autumn, his presence within that classroom had brought little to the children beyond unending noise and chaos, yet all of the complaints of children and parents and even the stated dissatisfaction of the Principal had not been able to effect a change. Now at last, somehow, after about five months, he was leaving. But, in his place, the school system did not have the wisdom to send in anyone more qualified. Instead of a confident or experienced instructor, there arrived first a bashful and terrified young lady and then, after her departure, a string of substitute teachers who seemed at times truly to have been dragged off the street at seven-thirty, handed a twenty-dollar bill, and shipped over to our school-house in a taxi. Some of them were nice people but few had any kind of apparent qualification. Anyone who looked once into that hectic classroom and then at these hapless teachers would have said in an instant that it was not likely to work out. Sending these teachers in here was as unthought-about, as uncalculated, as unplotted, as wholly whimsical, as unplanned, as it had been to send me into a school for discipline problems during my first weeks of teaching and without bothering to tell me the nature of the school.

So, in this case, the children were beginning to get some very strange specimens: one day a fellow who did not even arrive until about ten-thirty or eleven because he had been out driving a cab the night before and who announced, within about forty-five minutes, that he would certainly not be coming back. The consequence of all of this, in academic terms, was an overall retardation of almost the entire class of children, the few exceptions being those who were essentially being educated by their parents outside school. There was a chart on the wall that gave some measure of this by keeping a record of math and spelling grades. It was apparent from this that the math average of the children for weeks had remained, almost without exception, below the point of failing—and, for certain stretches of time, as much as thirty points below. Their spelling and their writing had fluctuated around the Third Grade level. Reading levels were a year, in many cases two years, behind the national norm. All of these were major tragedies because, in many respects, and for a number of the children, the stunting of their learning at such an early age was likely to prove almost irreversible. But the math and reading and spelling and writing, in one respect, were not as devastating setbacks for them as their work in social studies. For at least in the basic subject areas, and no matter how poorly they were doing, the children in that class had had some continuity of material and had done pretty much the same thing every day. In geography and history, there had not even been continuity, but rather a frantic and endless shifting of subject area, and consequently in those areas the children in the class were hopelessly mixed up.

One day a substitute teacher, groping for a way to kill an hour, would have the children read aloud to him about India. The next day, another teacher— not knowing or asking what had been done the day before, and maybe having a special fondness for another country, Holland perhaps—would tell the class to flip back a hundred pages and read about dikes and wooden shoes. Then someone would appear long enough to get some help from one of the full-time teachers and maybe the children would get two or three abortive sessions on the desert, but the day after that suddenly they would be doing India all over again, then off to Lima, Peru, suddenly to American cotton production, or the "corn belt" or "coal production"—or then, with the arrival of a new teacher, back to dikes and wooden shoes again. It is not surprising that, with a crazy arrangement of this sort, the children would frequently start out by lying to a new substitute and would do their best to destroy him and to break him down. Nor is it surprising that, after the course of such a year, their sense of place and time and even of self-localization would have been disastrously confused. They had no idea at all of the real relationships of different areas of the earth and could make no distinction, even in the most tentative and general manner, between a city, a town, a state, a country—or even a continent or island. Words like Yangtse River, Hemisphere, Nile, Himalayas, Pyramid, Ganges, Nomad, or Colorado were all inextricably mixed up in their minds. A question about what you can get from rushing streams in Switzerland might elicit such an answer as "population" or "migration" and a question about what "self-evident" means or "created equal" could easily bring back from the class such answers as "Red Coats," "transportation" or "white coal."

Seven different teachers in the course of ten days became the final catastrophe of this classroom. The children became wild, and the atmosphere from day to day grew more disturbing to the rest of the school. At this point, on the morning of the sixth of May, the Principal called me in to her office and asked me if I would agree to move across the hall and take that room. The idea was for one of the older teachers to take my own pupils and for me to take over the class of children who had been having such a time. With the assurance that my students would not be getting a string of substitutes, I agreed to make the transfer and I stayed up very late that night and the next day I went in to start with my new class.

I had a difficult time with that class of children for the first four or five days. It was almost as confusing and chaotic as the first days I had spent in the discipline school. Some of those mornings, I thought of myself as a row-boat going under in mid-ocean, the ocean being noise and cries and movements on all sides of me and all at almost the same time. During those days, I am sure I must have yelled and shouted at the children in that room as much as any teacher had ever done before and I probably scared some of them more than I should have. The point, though, is that I really did survive with them, and that I survived, in the end, in what I know now to have been the only good way: by which I mean that I saw the *class* survive and saw them not merely calm down but genuinely come to life again. I know, moreover, that it was not creating fear and shouting which did it, although that may have helped me to get through those first few days, but that it was something far more continuous and more important. The real reason that I was able to get on with those children in the state in which I found them is that I came into that room knowing myself to be absolutely on their side. I did not go in there with even the littlest suggestion that what had been going on that year was even one-fiftieth their fault. If I had done that, I am convinced that things would have been hopeless. I went in there, on the contrary, and in a manner that they soon detected, with loyalty only to them for their nerve and for their defiance and with an obvious and openly expressed dissatisfaction with the stupidity of a school system that had cheated them.

The first writing assignment that they passed in emphasized what many of those children were thinking and feeling. The assignment was to describe the way they felt about their school. As an alternative I said that, if they wanted, they could write about the street they lived on or about the whole neighborhood or about any other part of town. Because of the miserable state their writing was in, and out of a fear that they might not write anything at all if they felt they were going to be lambasted, I said that I wouldn't be looking at grammar or spelling or syntax in the beginning but that I would be looking for two things: (1) the richness and specificity of details and (2) the openness and courage with which they would put their own most private feelings down. Although I have taught all kinds of writing classes since then, I don't think that I ever again will receive such a trusting and wide-open reponse.

"In my school," began a paper that was handed back to me a few days later, "I see dirty boards and I see papers on the floor. I see an old browken window with a sign on it saying, Do not unlock this window are browken. And I see cracks in the walls and I see old books with ink poured all over them and I see old painting hanging on the walls. I see old alfurbet letter hanging on one nail on the wall. I see a dirty fire exit I see a old closet with supplys for the class. I see pigons flying all over the school. I see old freght trains throgh the fence of the school yard. I see pictures of contryies hanging on the wall and I see desks with wrighting all over the top of the desks and insited of the desk."

Another paper that was passed in to me said this: "There is a torn up house I live near and the stairs are broken down. The windows are boarded up too. One day I saw a little boy and his dog on the third floor. I don't know how they got up there but they were. The doors are pushed in and there is trash in the house dirt for it hasn't been clean for a long time. Everything is boarded up. The railing on the porch looks like it is going to fall off. One of the steps are about to fall off. Some children even go into the yard and on the porch of the house. The yard has glass, paper, rocks, broken pens and pencils, a torn dress, some pants, in it. It is the junkiest yard Ive ever seen. There is always a black cat in the yard too I never go near it though. I don't go into the yard but I look over my fence and I look into the house and yard."

Another child told me this: "I see lots of thinings in this room. I see new teachers omots every day. I can see flowers and children books and others things. I like the 100 papers I like allso cabnets. I don't like the drity windows. And the dusty window shallvalls . . ."

A little girl wrote this: "I can see old cars with gas in it and there is always people lighting fires old refrigartor an wood glass that comes from the old cars old trees and trash old weeds and people put there old chairs in there an flat tires and one thing there is up there is wood that you can make dog houses and there are beautiful flowers and there are dead dogs and cats . . . On some of the cars the weel is of and wisey bottles beer cans car seats are all out cars are all tip over and just the other day there was a fire and it was just blasting and whew in the back there is a big open space where Girl Scouts could mabe cook . . . this feild was a gas staition and the light pole is still up."

This was one more: "I see pictures in my school. I see pictures of Spain and a pictures of Portofino and a pictures of Chicago. I see arithmetic paper a spellings paper. I see a star chart. I see the flag of our Amerrica. The room is dirty . . . The auditorium dirty the seats are dusty. The light in the auditorium is brok. The curtains in the auditorium are ragged they took the curtains down because they was so ragged. The bathroom is dirty sometime the toilet is very hard. The cellar is dirty the hold school is dirty sometime . . . The flowers are dry every thing in my school is so so dirty."

When these essays were passed in, I showed one of them to the Reading Teacher. She became very angry. Her first reaction, which was expressed soon after I had handed her the essay, was to accuse me of having somehow concocted or coaxed this writing out of the child, whoever it was, who had composed it. "You must have induced it," she said, or "suggested it" or "invited it" or something like that, which was a way of disqualifying totally the independent intelligence and perception of the child who did the writing, at the same time that it discredited the impartiality and honesty of the teacher who could have allowed such thoughts to find their way to paper. What she said to me, essentially, was that I must have planted such gloomy word-pictures in the minds of the children or else they could not conceivably have written such things down. I was, on the contrary, very happy and quite proud of the children's essays because they were so direct and open and also so much filled with details. It was, I suppose, correct that in a sense I *had* induced this writing by telling the class to really go out and look at things and not write about their neighborhood or their school or about anything as if it were iden-

tical with the ingredients of the world or neighborhood that was often depicted in the pictures of
their books. The Reading Teacher also was probably
correct in saying that the children wouldn't have
written those essays if I hadn't said what I did because, as I have already shown, the great majority
had been thoroughly disciplined into the same kind
of pretense which the teachers themselves had
adopted for self-comfort; and this was a pretense
which did not allow for broken cars and boarded
windows. Another of the children's essays just started
off and announced that in September they had begun with such and such a teacher and then had
had so and so, and then so and so, and then so and
so, and right on through a list of about eight or
nine teachers ending up finally with me. It was cold-
blooded, factual, showed a good memory and was
shatteringly effective simply by rattling off almost
the entire list without making any pointed comments. This again she may or may not have done
if she hadn't been told she *could* do it, because the
general atmosphere at school militated against a photographic frankness of that sort.

The Reading Teacher was upset by this, by which-
ever of the essays it was that I showed her, but
rather than coming to terms with it by moving
toward the center of the problem and by asking
how the curriculum and tone of the school program
fitted in with such a picture of this child's life,
the Reading Teacher instead was able to handle
the child's honesty by pointing out to me that I
had probably angled for this, or induced it or
coaxed it or had been looking for it anyway—the last
of which charges possibly held a grain of truth but
did not have a thing to do with the problems that
the essays posed for her. The crux of it, I suppose,
is that this woman, like many other teachers, had
worked hard to develop and to solidify a set of optimistic values. To perpetrate the same views upon her

pupils therefore was not to lie to them (for her), at
least not consciously, but to extend to them, to
attempt really to "sell" to them, her own hard-
earned hopes about the world. During a long career
she had had a great deal of apparent success in in-
ducing the children she taught to write cheery and
pastel little letters and stories and book reports to
correspond to her own views. The reason the essays
written by my pupils were bound to be disturbing to
her was that she either deeply knew, or at least
faintly feared, that they were true.

There was another example of something like this
at one point a little earlier in the year. On one
wall of the section of the auditorium where the
Reading Teacher took her pupils, there was a list
which I once took the time to copy down. What the
list amounted to was a collection of suggested adjectives for the children to try to use when they were
doing book reports. I remember that I studied the
list and later discussed it with the Reading Teacher
because there was something quite remarkable about
it: All of the adjectives were laudatory. Everything
that they implied was something nice. "Humorous"
and "interesting" and "comical" and "adventurous"
were typical of the words which were recommended
to the children by virtue of being included in this
list. There wasn't one that left room for even partial criticism. As these were the adjectives which the
children were being asked to use, the consequence,
except in the case of a rare intellectual accident,
would have had to be a book report that spoke only
in terms of various kinds of "good." Since we know
that not all books are good, and in fact that many
books are bad, and since we know in particular that
many of the books at school were poor, that some
were really rotten and that only a handful, probably
only a very slim minority were books of any real
quality at all, and since, beyond that (and this
seems much more important) even a book that

seems good to one person, to a teacher or to one pupil, may very likely seem poor to another pupil, and be poor for him, and for some very good reason too—for all of these reasons I was curious about the effect of this list of laudatory adjectives which had faded upon the wall from what I believe to have been many years of use.

I remember a day when I was reading in the auditorium with a small group of children. We were reading, out of the phonics book *Wide Doors Open,* a story which none of them seemed to like very much and several were yawning the whole while. The Reading Teacher's manner of handling this would have been to attempt to "sell" it to the children, to call it wonderful and to sweep over them with a wave of persuasive enthusiasm in order to make up for their resistance to the work. I did not see why I ought to do this or why I ought to try to force upon them an appreciation of a type of story which they did not like. The story that we were reading was for some good reason of no importance to them and I was not going to try to persuade them it was terrific when they did not feel it. When we were done with the story I asked them whether they had liked it, and the thing that astonished me was that almost every one of them pretended that he *had.* I said: "What did you think of it? How would you describe it? What kind of story was it?" The answers came back: "Interesting"—"humorous" —"colorful"—"adventurous"—and all of the rest of the words on the Reading Teacher's list.

I twisted my head and I looked up at the list in the back of the room. There they all were. The words that they had given me were all up in neat order on the permissible list. They had not even begun thinking. They had not even started responding. They had simply assumed that, because I had asked the question, one of those words must be the right answer. The terrible thought that there *was* a right

answer and that I already *knew* it and that it remained only for them to *guess* it was most disheartening of all. I remember that when they suggested
each adjective it was not in a voice which said "I
think it was humorous"—or "I think it was adventurous"—or "I think it was interesting"—or any
other kind of definitive assertion of opinion. Rather,
it was all phrased as a kind of guessing-game to
which there was one answer: "Humorous?" "Adventurous?" "Interesting?" "Comical?" It was all in
the interrogative and the effort was all to find out
what I, their teacher, had already decided to be
true. Finally, irritated and a little angry, I asked
them flatly: "What are you telling me? You've all
been yawning and twisting. Why didn't you pay attention if all of those wonderful things were so?"

One boy answered me simply, as if there were no
contradiction between this and the use of the other
words: "Because it was so babyish." Then how on
earth could they have used all of the words on the
Reading Teacher's list? Another boy said: "It was so
boring." So there the real answer was. It seemed
obvious why they had lied to me in the beginning.
The Reading Teacher had taught them that those
were the only things you were supposed to say
about a book. One of them, one of those adjectives,
was "correct" and the only problem for them was to
find out which one it was. The word, all too clearly,
had been divorced from the world, and the application of the correct pat adjective need have nothing
in particular to do with the child's idea about the
book.

I felt troubled enough about this to relate it later
to the Reading Teacher. Just as with the essays by the
children that I had shown her, I felt she was immediately disturbed by what she was hearing but I
also recognized that she was very quick to cancel it
out. She seemed troubled for a moment but then,
instead of saying that it was a pity, or that it was

funny but regrettable, or too bad that they had reacted in such a manner, or anything else at all that might have brought her doubt or pause, she said only this:

"At least it shows that they know the words on the list."

What I felt when she said that, was that knowing all those big words on the list would not be of any use. It would not be of any use because they could not work with them but could only "supply" them, fetch them out literally from their place on the list, in much the same manner that a young dog fetches a thrown stick. By reassuring herself that at least the children had gotten down those big words for future use, the Reading Teacher was able to rise above the painful matter that she had effectively taught them to be good liars and in fact had equipped them with a set of tools to keep themselves at as far as possible a distance from the truth.

Rather than learn those ten-dollar words, the introduction of which into their book reports might win them such rewards as gold stars and extra points, the children would have gained greatly from having been invited to search their own barrel of modifiers, containing such words as "boring," "horrible," "terrible," "great," "pathetic," "idiotic," "terrific," "marvelous" or "dumb." These are the kinds of strong words which are looked for by good college English instructors in their efforts at erasing the use of the kinds of cliché terms listed above. But what process of education is it which would inculcate these very unnatural "cultured words" at the age of ten only to have to define their artificiality and point up their lack of vitality and attempt in many cases to root them out only ten years later?

I remember the Reading Teacher on one occasion asking a child for the antonym of "fat" and getting "skinny." The Reading Teacher's response was something on this order: "Oh let's see if we can't find a nicer word than skinny"—and getting "thin" and "slender" in its place. A decade later, if that child made it to college, I thought, her English teacher would work his heart out trying to get "skinny" back again.

At one point later in the spring, the Deputy Superintendent, Miss Sullivan, went on record as indicating that she held it a key goal of the Boston Public Schools to break the children of Roxbury of what she called their "speech patterns." There is no way to be absolutely certain of what she intended, but if the Deputy Superintendent meant by this process the replacement of words like "skinny" by such a word as "thin" or "slender," then I think that she may very well succeed in enabling some of the children to speak more like herself but I do not believe that she will have helped them toward expressing themselves richly or with any kind of honesty or strength. Honest writing and private feeling seem to me to be the only possible starting-points for everything else in teaching English and one of the first places where the world outside and the word within the classroom ought to eloquently co-exist. To bring about this kind of a meeting would not be easy in much of the present Boston school system, but it would be education.

SIXTEEN

ONE of my first responsibilities after starting with my new pupils was to make a detailed check-list of all the books in the room. The list had to include how many copies of each book were available, as well as the date of publication, author and publisher of each. When the list was done, I was obliged to pass it in, but fortunately I thought of taking it out of school first and having it photostated.

The list indicates that there were thirty-two book series available in multiple copies in the classroom. Of these, six series were five years old or newer. Seven were between five and ten years old. Seven fell into the category of ten to fifteen years old, five into the category of fifteen to twenty years old, and seven into the category of twenty to thirty-five years old. It is probably true that many of these older books were not intended to be used any longer and also it is true that a couple of the very oldest series existed in only a handful of copies each. Nonetheless, I think the general tone and feeling of the school may well be imagined from the overall fact that, of those series which were made available to the children, seven were published before the bombing of Hiroshima and 60 per cent were at that moment over ten years old. In terms of numbers of copies, rather than of book series, there were a total of 606 books within the room. Of this total, the number of copies that were ten years old or newer was 303. Of the rest, 121 books were more than twenty years old. In terms of appearance, as well as of real newness of content, as opposed to a merely revised edition of something inherently archaic and dead, there were probably only a handful of books in the room that any fair observer would have called really new.

Another fact that comes across from the comprehensive booklist is that, among all the book series, only three existed in thirty-four or more copies. One was the biography series *Heroes, Heroines, and Holidays*, of which there were thirty-five copies, another was the Laidlaw *Great Names in American History*, of which there were thirty-four, and the third was the Thorndike-Barnhart dictionary, of which there were thirty-six copies. The reason these figures are astonishing is that the class size during most of the year numerically exceeded the number of books in the various series. What this meant was that, whenever a class was being taught to all the children, at least two or three, more likely five or six or seven, would have had to double up or go without a book. In some cases this may have afforded no problem since a couple of the children, as I have said, were special students and it was probably not even intended that they have books since nobody seriously expected them to be learning anything. In a great majority of cases, however, if a new teacher (for example, a new substitute) should have come into the room and attempted to do a regular geography or spelling or science or math lesson with even three-quarters of the students, he would still have run into immediate trouble in the matter of participation and unknowingly would have been forced to leave half a dozen children out. At times this problem might be solved in a haphazard fashion by hunting around for the book of a child who was not at school. The chaos involved in this, however, and the waste of time, may be imagined—not to speak of the overall indignity and lack of respect for ownership on the part of any single child. In too many cases the lesson would take place and it would be nearly over, before the teacher would recognize that a whole group of children sitting in the back row had not had any book.

It is true that, in addition to all the books I have listed, there also were programmed reading materials available in the building, and these materials were somewhat more modern than the antiquated texts. Yet even these, while offering the advantage of programming, had made only the most slender accommodation to the deeper changes in the times. Of 144 separate selections available in one programmed kit, for example, there were two that made a half-hearted accommodation to liberal pressure by being either about Negro people or else the work of Negro authors. This was a recognizable improvement over the biographical series in the cupboard but it still seemed less than adequate.

A more basic problem, however—and one that makes the whole question of the possible merit of the programmed kit irrelevant in this case—is the fact that the teacher who had been in that room most of the year had botched the use of it. The children had been taught to use the kit incorrectly and the answers they gave were generally invalidated. The self-checking system had also been confused. For this reason, if the kit was "programming" anything for those children, it programmed retardation. To watch those lessons taking place back in December had been a full-fledged nightmare: children leaping up, writing in the wrong spaces, checking with the wrong answers, tearing out whole pages, the teacher sweating, miserable, hectic—and the brighter students sitting silently as usual, but looking truly as though they were about to jump out of their skins. The very name of the reading-kit had by now become so poisonous to the children that they did not want to use it or even hear about it.

The other major source of literary material for use at school was the large volume called the "Course of Study." This was written by teachers and put together under Miss Sullivan's supervision. The copy that I had bore a printing date of 1959. The book set out with good intentions.

These are some of the first words:

"The classroom is the child's home for many hours each day. It is also his place of work. Therefore, the classroom should reflect the happiness, the protection, the loving guidance of the home, as well as the efficiency of the workshop . . . In addition to consideration for the physical welfare and intellectual advancement of the child, an atmosphere of culture must permeate the teaching scene."

These sentiments are undoubtedly well-meant, even if they seem rather automatic. The dedication to "the physical welfare and intellectual advancement" of the child, however, must be placed side by side with the physical realities of the actual school buildings, and the "atmosphere of culture" which is to "permeate the teaching scene" has to be placed side by side with some examples of what the school system really means by culture. I think it is found, as soon as we look at some examples, that "cultural" in these writings becomes something very close to "cheery" or "hopeful" or "positive" or "optimistic" —and, therefore, a great deal of the time, with "artificial." The fact that such a definition is bound to be unrealistic to the children of a ghetto, as well as being unfaithful to art and not very responsive to truth, has gone entirely by the board.

The section of the Course of Study that contains the poetry selections is briefly prefaced by these words:

"Children like poetry because they are sensitive to rhythm and music and are attracted by its brevity and directness. They are always eager to learn more about the world in which they live . . . The enjoyment of a poem is enhanced by the timeliness of its presentation. Circumstances and interests affect the reception children will accord a poem . . . The lists of poems presented . . . offer a wide choice for each grade. These lists may be extended to include the presentation of other worthwhile poems." The preface also tells the teacher that "the emotional experience" of a poem will be heightened for a class if he takes thought, in his choice of work and presentation, of "relating the theme of the poem to the child's experience." I would like to look now at some examples of the material recommended in the Course of Study in order to see to what extent these recommendations are either serious or possible.

"Dare to be right!" says one of these selections, by an author who is designated only as Anonymous, "Dare to be true: The failings of others can never save you. Stand by your conscience, your honor, your faith; Stand like a hero, and battle till death." Another quotation that is recommended is by a person bearing the name of Susan Coolidge: "Every day is a fresh beginning, Every morn is the world made anew; You who are weary of sorrow and sinning, Here is a beautiful hope for you—A hope for me and a hope for you." A person who is described only as Faber wrote these words: "For right is right, since God is God, And right the day must win; To doubt would be disloyalty, To falter would be sin." Another, by somebody named C. B. Searles: "Christmas, Christmas, blessed name, To rich and poor you mean the same—In every land beneath the sun All Christian hearts just think as one." Another is by a poet bearing the name of P. F. Freeman: "There is beauty in the sunshine An' clouds that roam the sky; there is beauty in the Heavens, An' the stars that shine on high. There is beauty in the moonbeams That shine both pale an' fair—An' it matters not where'er we go There is beauty everywhere."

The poems above are not by famous people. There are other poems in the selections, however, which are the work of known authors but whose appearance here, whether due to bad choices or excision out of context or the company of the other material, becomes degrading and embarrassing to the names which are attached to them. "So here hath been dawning Another blue day," is attributed to Carlyle: "Think, wilt thou let it Slip useless away?" Emerson: "Not gold, but only men, can make A people great and strong; Men, who for Truth and Honor's sake, Stand fast and suffer long." Tennyson: "Howe'er it be, it seems to me 'Tis only noble to be good. Kind hearts are more than coronets, And simple faith than Norman blood." Belloc: "Of Courtesy, it is much less Than Courage of Heart or Holiness, Yet in my walks it seems to me That the Grace of God is Courtesy." Characteristic of these poems, mingling good feeling, moralism and old-fashioned beneficence, is the following little verse by a lesser known poet bearing the name of Alexander Smart: "Better than grandeur, better than gold, Than rank or titles, a hundred-fold, Is a healthy body, and a mind at ease, And simple pleasures that always please. A heart that can feel for a neighbor's woe, And share in his joy with a friendly glow, With sympathies large enough to infold, All men as brothers, is better than gold."

Reading all of this material together, it is easy enough to become condescending and sarcastic. Perhaps sarcasm and condescension are even called for in the face of material which is so poor, but they are no more useful and no more helpful than it would have been to make fun of the speaking style of an old man like Joseph Lee. What seems useful is to ask, not so much how this poetry fits with a particular adult reader's standard of good literature, as how it is going to sit with the real-life world and honest reaction of an eight- or ten-, or even twelve- or fourteen-year-old child. I am afraid that, on all counts, it is going to fall down. The following incident may illustrate a part of what I mean:

One day in the previous autumn (of 1964), when I was still a substitute teacher being shuttled about from school to school, I was sent in to the highly explosive Patrick Campbell Junior High. I was given as my assignment a class of Eighth Grade children who were designated problem students because they were either of very low intelligence or else emotionally disturbed. The class, mostly Negro, included some of the poorest children in the city and they were in one of the worst single junior highs, if not the worst one, in the area. The boys, for some reason, were gone much of the morning, so that I was working mainly with about a dozen girls. In their desks several of those girls had small transistor radios which they would tune in at moments when I wasn't looking to pick up the local stations that broadcast rock and roll. Most of the girls were physically grown up. Their regular teacher, of whom they spoke without affection, had chalked up on the blackboard a poem that I remember as having been by Edgar Guest. It may have been by someone else and it may not even have been in the Course of Study but, whatever poem it was, it seemed typical of the sort of poem which is in the Course of Study and it was about nature, as I remember, about autumn, about some leaves, about a tree. It had to do with those subjects and I remember asking one of the children, and then some others, if they would say it for me.

One girl read it and then another, and perhaps a few others, and I thought that I had seldom heard anything so hollow and so empty and so redolent of boredom in my life. I asked the children what the poem was about, and none could say. Neither, honestly, in any important sense could I. It was obvious that for these Negro girls—dead-end students already in a dreadful, gloomy, tenth-rate junior high —the idea of poetry, when it meant anything at all, had something to do with big words that you could say in a singsong, recite to show you are a good girl, and do not even attempt to understand. The possibility of its having anything at all to do with your own life or sufferings, or with your own joys and exaltations, was not even in the picture.

That morning in the junior high school I read to the girls in that classroom about half a dozen poems by the Negro poet Langston Hughes. When I held up the book and they saw its new cover, that alone was appealing, for very few new and crisp and fresh-looking volumes ever got in to desecrate those rooms. On the cover they saw the picture of a Negro author, and they commented on that. Their comments had to do with a single, obvious, overriding fact: *"Look—that man's colored."*

I made a tape-recording of part of my morning in that class. No transistor radios reappeared or were turned on during that next hour and, although some of the children interrupted me a lot to quiz me about Langston Hughes, where he was born, whether he was rich, whether he was married, and about poetry, and about writers, and writing in general, and a number of other things that struck their fancy, and although it also was not a calm or orderly or, above all, disciplined class by traditional definition and there were probably very few minutes in which you would have been able to hear a pin drop or hear my reading uninterrupted by the voices of one or another of the girls, at least I did have their attention and they seemed, if anything, to care only too much about the content of that Negro poet's book. I felt uncertain while I was with them, and not at all sure if I was really getting anywhere or not. But, when I came home, I played back the tape and I recognized that it had been an extraordinary day. Since that time I have sometimes met two or three of the children who were students in that class. All of them remember the green book of poetry that I read with them that day and, while most of them forget the name of the man who wrote the poetry, they remember the names of the poems he wrote, and they remember something else. They remember that he was Negro.

SEVENTEEN

THERE is a booklet published by the Boston Public Schools and bearing the title "A Curriculum Guide in Character Education." This booklet was in the desk of my new classroom and so, as few things are explicitly stated to you and so much must be done by guessing within these poorly run schools, I made the guess that I was supposed to look at it and perhaps make use of it. I did look at it but I did not make use of it. I kept it, however, and studied it and I have it in front of me now.

The booklet, really, is little more than an anthology broken down according to the values which the Boston School Committee hopes to instill or inspire in a child. This is the list of character traits which the teacher is encouraged to develop in a child:

"CHARACTER TRAITS TO BE DEVELOPED: OBEDIENCE TO DULY CONSTITUTED AUTHORITY . . . SELF-CONTROL . . . RESPONSIBILITY . . . GRATITUDE . . . KINDNESS . . . GOOD WORKMANSHIP AND PERSEVERANCE . . . LOYALTY . . . TEAMWORK . . . HONESTY . . . FAIR PLAY."

Two of the things that seem most striking about this list are (1) the emphasis upon obedience characteristics and (2) the way in which the personality has been dissected and divided and the way in which consequently each "character trait" has been isolated and dwelt upon in the manner of a list of favorable characteristics in the eulogy at a funeral or in the citation of an honorary degree during a commencement ceremony. You look in vain through this list for anything that has to do with an original child or with an independent style. You also look in vain for any evaluation or assessment or conception of the human personality as a full or organic or continuously living and evolving firmament rather than as a filing cabinet of acceptable traits.

The section on obedience characteristics begins with the following verse: "We must do the thing we must Before the thing we may; We are unfit for any trust Till we can and do obey." It goes on to list the forms that obedience can take and it recommends a list of "selected memory gems" having to do with compliance to authority. Some of them are good and some are by famous people, but all of them, coming at you this way, out of context, have a killing, dull effect. They come one after another, some good, some dumb, and leave you feeling very obedient:

Honor thy father and thy mother [is the first one]. He who knows how to obey will know how to command . . . Obedience to God is the best evidence of sincere love for Him . . . True obedience is true liberty . . . The good American obeys the laws . . . Help me to be faithful to my country, careful for its good, valiant for its defense, and obedient to its laws . . . He who would command others must first learn to obey . . . The first law that ever God gave to man was a law of obedience . . . My son Hannibal will be a great general, because of all my soldiers he best knows how to obey . . . Obedience sums up our entire duty . . . The first great law is to obey . . . Children, obey your parents in all things; for this is well pleasing to the Lord . . . Wicked men obey from fear; good men from love . . . We are born subjects and to obey God is perfect liberty. He that does this shall be free, safe, and happy . . . Obedience is not truly performed by the body if the heart is dissatisfied . . . Every day, in every way it is our duty to obey. "Every way" means prompt and willing, Cheerfully, each task fulfilling. It means, too, best work achieving Habits of obedi-

ence, weaving. To form a cable firm and strong
With links unbreakable and long: To do a thing, at
once, when told A blessing, doth the act enfold.
Obedience, first to God, we owe; It should in all
our actions show . . . If you're told to do a thing,
And mean to do it really, Never let it be by halves,
Do it fully, freely! Do not make a poor excuse
Waiting, weak, unsteady; All obedience worth the
name Must be prompt and ready.

Of all the quotations included in this list, I think
there are only two which are deeply relevant to the
case at hand: "Wicked men obey from fear; good
men from love"—this comes from Aristotle. And:
"Obedience is not truly performed by the body if
the heart is dissatisfied," which comes from the Tal-
mudic scholar Saadia. Both of these quotations are
directly applicable to the exact problem exemplified
by the kind of school system in which such a list
could be seriously employed. If it is true, as Aristotle
wrote, that wicked men obey from fear and good
men from love, then where else is this more likely to
become manifest than within these kinds of peni-
tential schools? One thinks of the pathos of anxiety
with which teachers and principals go about their
duties, seldom out of respect for their superiors,
which in so many cases is impossible, but out of an
abject fear of being condemned or of being kicked
out. I think of the Art Teacher confiding to me
in an excited whisper: "Can you imagine that this
principal honestly and truly can stand there and
call herself an educator? It's the biggest laugh of the
school year." The Reading Teacher, with equal
vehemence, talking about my supervisor: "That man
doesn't know as much about elementary education as
the first-year substitutes do. You'll have to agree to
whatever he says and then ignore it when he's gone."
To these people, whom they held in deeply justified
contempt, both women paid ample lip-service. If
ever they were honest, I do not see how they could

have avoided holding both themselves and each other
in some portion of the same contempt.

Saadia's eloquent statement that "obedience is not
truly performed by the body if the heart is dissatisfied" seems also appropriate to the Boston public
schools. For the heart *is* dissatisfied here, and the
obedience *is* perfunctory, and the whole concept of
respect for unearned and undeserved authority is
bitter and brittle and back-breaking to children,
whether rich or poor, or black or white, within
these kinds of schools. Only the authority of visible
character demands respect. No other kind deserves
it. No child in his heart, unless drugged by passivity,
will pay obeisance to authority unless authority
has earned it, and authority based upon political
maneuvering and upon the ingestion and assimilation of platitudes is an authority which no person, white or Negro, adult or child, should respect.
There is too much respect for authority in the Boston schools, and too little respect for the truth. If
there were more of the latter, there would be less
need of the former and the atmosphere of the Boston
schools would not have to be so nearly what it is
today: the atmosphere of a crumbling dictatorship
in time of martial law. The emphasis both in this
one booklet and in the words of the school administration in general upon the need for dumb obedience belies its deepest fear.

Another section of the "Character Education" booklet has to do with self-control:

"Teach the necessity for self-discipline by all people," the teacher is advised. "Guide the children
through discussion to recognize the necessity of self-
discipline . . . Responsible, self-disciplined people are
an asset to the community . . . People in a community should live by principle, not by emotion . . .
Emergencies are met by disciplined people, e.g.,
pilots, drivers, teachers, pioneers, policemen, fire-
fighters, doctors, nurses, American Red Cross work-

ers, clergymen, astronauts . . . Disciplined people make good neighbors . . ." The teacher is next told to "select many examples of self-disciplined people and discuss events in their lives which exemplify self-control, e.g., Abraham Lincoln, Louis Pasteur, Robert Fulton, Thomas Edison, Charles Lindbergh, Robinson Crusoe, Daniel Boone, George R. Clarke, Helen Keller, Florence Nightingale, Clara Barton, Dwight D. Eisenhower, Dr. Tom Dooley, Dr. Albert Schweitzer."

The unit on "good workmanship and perseverance" puts forth another list of famous men, several of them the same ones as before. The list in this case is notable partly for the odd discrepancies between the statures of the different people who are involved and partly, simply, for the heavy and thudding and skull-hammering manner in which the whole thing is gotten across:

Discuss the perseverance and good workmanship of 1. Individuals whose inventions have made our way of life easier, e.g., Gutenberg, Watts, Whitney, Bell, Edison, Howe, Wright. 2. Individuals whose research has made it possible for us to be safer from disease, e.g., Curie, Roentgen, Lister, Pasteur, Salk, Sabin. 3. Individuals who have shown good workmanship in spite of physical handicaps, e.g., Demosthenes, R. L. Stevenson, Helen Keller, Steinmetz, Dr. Tom Dooley, President Roosevelt, President Kennedy, Mayor John F. Collins. 4. Individuals whose artistry has provided us with pleasure, e.g., a. Music—Chopin, Mozart, Schubert, Leonard Bernstein, Arthur Feidler [sic], etc. b. Authors—Dickens, Anderson, Longfellow, Alcott, Stevenson, etc. c. Artists—Raphael, Michelangelo, Millet, Grandma Moses . . .

When I look at this list, I find myself wondering who on earth could ever have put it all together and I also wonder whether anyone really thinks that you are going to teach character, or anything, to children by rattling off a list of all the people in the world or in America or in Boston who have struggled to make good. "Like a postage stamp, a man's value depends on his ability to stick to anything until he gets there." This is quoted from someone by the name of Chamberlain. "Excellence is never granted to man, but is a reward of labor," is quoted from Reynolds. "Do the very best you can today and tomorrow you can do better," says someone named M. Vanbee. Can teachers and children be expected to take this seriously? And who is it who bears responsibility for this soul-drowning dreariness and waste of hours? With material as bad as this, surely it is no wonder that the matter of motivation has become such an overriding factor in the considerations of those who administer these schools. It cannot be unexpected that motivation becomes the all-important obstacle when the material is so often a diet of banality and irrelevance which it is not worth the while of a child to learn or that of a teacher to teach.

This seems to be a central issue. For the problem of motivation is talked about endlessly in Boston, and the point has been made repeatedly in the writings of Miss Sullivan and others that the motivational difficulty has its origin in the children and in their backgrounds, rather than in the teachers or the schools. I think the opposite is true. But the predictability with which this wrong assertion has been restated suggests the nervousness which the school administration of this city must experience in regard to its own failure.

"How can we motivate these culturally deprived in-migrant minorities to learn?"

This is the form of the standard question. The blame, in almost all cases, is immediately placed upon the child's background and his family. Then, but only after it has divested itself of prior responsibility, does the school administration come forward to profess a willingness to do what it can. Miss Sullivan, for example, in putting forward the aims of the compensatory program designed for Negro children, presented such an attitude in the following words: This endeavor, she said, "is a preventive program designed to catch undesirable situations in their incipiency, to improve children's attitudes toward school, to inspire standards of excellence which should be carried over into secondary education for all and beyond for many. It is our hope through this program to raise the achievement of these pupils closer to their potentials which have for too long been submerged by parental lack of values."

The last phrase is a defensive one. It suggests that the child will be granted full mercy, high pardon and even a certain amount of compassion just so long as it is made absolutely clear ahead of time that the heart of the problem is the lack of values of his parents. I don't think that the Negro parents lack values. I think the people who administer the Boston school system do. To go a bit further, honestly, I do not understand what is implied by such a phrase as "the lack of values" of the culturally deprived. I think that when we are faced with an expression of that kind, we have to ask whose values we are talking about and "deprived" in the eyes of whom? To say that Negroes in Boston are deprived of rights would be an honest statement. It would also be honest to say that they are deprived of good schools and that, along with this, they are deprived of a fair chance, of democracy, of opportunity, and of all the things these words are supposed to mean. But to say that they are deprived culturally, in the face of Boston's School Superintendent, in the face of Mrs. Hicks, in the face of the profound cynicism of the entire system, seems to me meaningless. The phrase "cultural deprivation" has not met with a great deal of favor among Negroes and is, as a consequence, going out of fashion quickly with white

liberals. Needless to say, it is still a fervent catch-
cry in the Boston schools.

Edgar Friedenberg has written recently that the
education and assimilation of Negro people provide
American society with one of its last chances "to
transfuse into itself a stream of people whose moral
vision has been—relatively, at least—preserved and
sharpened by exclusion from opportunities for self-
betrayal as well as self-advancement." If people regret, as some must, the exclusion of Negroes from
opportunities for advancement, there is at least reason to be grateful for an equal exclusion from opportunities for self-betrayal. Too many white people in Boston are compromised, to the point of seeming almost impotent, because they have been, not by
others, but by themselves essentially betrayed. There
is also the problem of those who, having grown up
in low status, are determined, once their head is a
little bit above water, to make the next generation
of unlucky people pay. One man at my school, the
redneck teacher I have quoted often, once said to
me in his usual frankness that he had been beaten
all around and treated rough and whipped and so
on by his parents or teachers or both when he had
been a child. To him, this seemed to clear the field
for beating others around today. The attitude of
many older people in our school system has been
consistent with this view: "We had a hard time of
it, so why shouldn't they?" This less than gentle attitude is characteristic of a less than gentle city in
which the overriding outlook of those who are moderately successful is too likely to be that they have
got theirs and the others can damn well wait a
while before they get the same. Friedenberg has
also written in a somewhat different context that
former prisoners make bad jailers. A corollary to
this is that former slum-residents make poor landlords. And former Irish boys beaten by Yankee school-
masters may frequently make ungenerous teachers

for little boys whose skins are black. The matter of where the real values lie seems to me to be the final important question of this book.

You can't, obviously, say things like this without bringing down professional resentment on your head. In a school system like Boston's, where there is so little inward credential for service, the outward credential counts for a great deal. For the lack of such credentials, therefore, any straightforward critic is apt to be condemned. Ushers take their usher-uniforms seriously. In Boston, teachers take their degrees and accumulated credits seriously and administrators take their political positions as a palliation for their inward sense of empty space. Mechanical credentials make up for genuine ones in this system and it is precisely in this manner that fragile bureaucracies have often defended themselves and their areas of power from the dangers of real life. That same blunt redneck teacher at my school who spoke with so much honesty on most topics once made this remark to me while we were chatting:

"They talk about the Negroes being culturally deprived. I'm the one who's been goddamn culturally deprived and I don't need anyone to tell me. I haven't learned a thing, read a thing, that I wished I'd read or learned since the day I entered high school, and I've known it for years and I tried to hide it from myself and now I wish I could do something about it but I'm afraid it's just too late."

Few people in Boston have the openness to talk that way. The man who spoke those words will probably be a principal some day. I think he will probably be a much better principal than most, if for no other reason than that he knows so well what he is lacking. But how many other people in our city will ever allow themselves even that degree of insight? And how many of those others, who may have the superficial trappings and the polysyllables of "culture," will ever stop to think of some of the deeper and truer things that culture ought to be about?

One day, during the first weeks of May of 1965, I received at last a visit in my classroom from the lady who has had so large a role in defining the application and the limitations of the word "culture" within the Boston schools. It was about a week after I had started work with my new students. I looked up from my desk, or from whatever I had been doing, and I realized that the personage known as Marguerite Sullivan was standing at the door. The children stared at her, as I did also—a bit awed by her appearance.

The lady we saw before us was an unusually tall woman with an authoritative and rather pleasant face. She came into the classroom, smiled very broadly at the children and waited for them to scramble out of their seats and say "Good morning" to her. She told them that she did not think that they said it with very much energy and so she asked them to say it once more. That time, she beamed at them very warmly and said in a hopeful and cheery old-fashioned voice: "Oh! what cultured children!" after which the children could sit down. Miss Sullivan's next act was to turn to me and to praise me flamboyantly, for what I did not know since she had not seen me for thirty seconds, and the Principal next spoke to Miss Sullivan, in my hearing, as to the possibility of my being in the school again the following year despite my lack of education courses. Miss Sullivan said surely there must be a way to use me, and by all of this I was more than a little perplexed because, as I have said, I had scarcely been observed by the Deputy Superintendent but already I was being treated in a very flattering warm style. When a compliment like that is based upon a total lack of information it seems like a kind of mockery. We all know, children too, when we are being complimented falsely, as by a mechanism of

bureaucratic ingratiation. In such a case, honest insult, based upon fact, would make us feel more comfortable.

A few minutes later, in a classroom across the
hall from mine, a teacher whose class was a little
unruly was addressed by Miss Sullivan in a very
different style: "Not very good discipline, girlie!"
Miss Sullivan said it to her right in front of the
whole class. The teacher later, in the cellar, was re-
duced to tears. The Deputy Superintendent's praise
or insult, just like her words about my class being
so "cultured," seemed to have no connection to her
knowledge of the facts. She was evidently so accus-
tomed to the total deployment of her autocracy that
anything that came to her mind seemed justified in
being put forth, even when she could not have had
enough information to make a decent judgment. I
therefore felt no exhilaration about the way she
spoke to me, even though what she had said was
flattering. Mostly, I believe that I just felt angry and
offended at the way that she had thrown the hundred-
dollar word "cultured" at my children. For the kind
of culture that they honestly did have was something
that she did not respect, and was not even willing
to acknowledge, while the kind of thing that she
seemed to mean by culture was something that I
would have given everything in my power to protect
them from.

EIGHTEEN

PERHAPS a reader would like to know what it is like to go into a new classroom in the same way that I did and to see before you suddenly, and in terms you cannot avoid recognizing, the dreadful consequences of a year's wastage of real lives.

You walk into a narrow and old wood-smelling classroom and you see before you thirty-five curious, cautious and untrusting children, aged eight to thirteen, of whom about two-thirds are Negro. Three of the children are designated to you as special students. Thirty per cent of the class is reading at the Second Grade level in a year and in a month in which they should be reading at the height of Fourth Grade performance or at the beginning of the Fifth. Seven children out of the class are up to par. Ten substitutes or teacher changes. Or twelve changes. Or eight. Or eleven. Nobody seems to know how many teachers they have had. Seven of their lifetime records are missing: symptomatic and emblematic at once of the chaos that has been with them all year long. Many more lives than just seven have already been wasted but the seven missing records become an embittering symbol of the lives behind them which, equally, have been lost or mislaid. (You have to spend the first three nights staying up until dawn trying to reconstruct these records out of notes and scraps.) On the first math test you give, the class average comes out to 36. The children tell you with embarrassment that it has been like that since fall.

You check around the classroom. Of forty desks, five have tops with no hinges. You lift a desk-top to fetch a paper and you find that the top has fallen off. There are three windows. One cannot be opened. A sign on it written in the messy scribble of a hurried teacher or some custodial person warns you: DO NOT UNLOCK THIS WINDOW IT IS BROKEN. The general look of the room is as of a bleak-light photograph of a mental hospital. Above the one poor blackboard, gray rather than really black, and hard to write on, hangs from one tack, lopsided, a motto attributed to Benjamin Franklin: *"Well begun is half done."* Everything, or almost everything like that, seems a mockery of itself.

Into this grim scenario, drawing on your own pleasures and memories, you do what you can to bring some kind of life. You bring in some cheerful and colorful paintings by Joan Miro and Paul Klee. While the paintings by Miro do not arouse much interest, the ones by Klee become an instantaneous success. One picture in particular, a watercolor titled "Bird Garden," catches the fascination of the entire class. You slip it out of the book and tack it up on the wall beside the doorway and it creates a traffic jam every time the children have to file in or file out. You discuss with your students some of the reasons why Klee may have painted the way he did and you talk about the things that can be accomplished in a painting which could not be accomplished in a photograph. None of this seems to be above the children's heads. Despite this, you are advised flatly by the Art Teacher that your naïveté has gotten the best of you and that the children cannot possibly appreciate this. Klee is too difficult. Children will not enjoy it. You are unable to escape the idea that the Art Teacher means herself instead.

For poetry, in place of the recommended memory gems, going back again into your own college days, you make up your mind to introduce a poem of William Butler Yeats. It is about a lake isle called Innisfree, about birds that have the funny name of "linnets" and about a "bee-loud glade." The children do not all go crazy about it but a number of them seem to like it as much as you do and you tell them how once, three years before, you were living in England and you helped a man in the country to make his home from wattles and clay. The children become intrigued. They pay good attention and many of them grow more curious about the poem than they appeared at first. Here again, however, you are advised by older teachers that you are making a mistake: Yeats is too difficult for children. They can't enjoy it, won't appreciate it, wouldn't like it. You are aiming way above their heads . . . Another idea comes to mind and you decide to try out an easy and rather well-known and not very complicated poem of Robert Frost. The poem is called "Stopping By Woods on a Snowy Evening." This time, your supervisor happens to drop in from the School Department. He looks over the mimeograph, agrees with you that it's a nice poem, then points out to you —tolerantly, but strictly—that you have made another mistake. "Stopping By Woods" is scheduled for Sixth Grade. It is not "a Fourth Grade poem," and it is not to be read or looked at during the Fourth Grade. Bewildered as you are by what appears to be a kind of idiocy, you still feel reproved and criticized and muted and set back and you feel that you have been caught in the commission of a serious mistake.

On a series of other occasions, the situation is repeated. The children are offered something new and something lively. They respond to it energetically and they are attentive and their attention does not waver. For the first time in a long while perhaps there is actually some real excitement and some growing and some thinking going on within that one small room. In each case, however, you are advised sooner or later that you are making a mistake. Your mistake, in fact, is to have impinged upon the standardized condescension on which the entire administration of the school is based. To hand Paul Klee's pictures to the children of this classroom, and particularly in a twenty-dollar volume, constitutes a threat to this school system. It is not different from sending a little girl from the Negro ghetto into an art class near Harvard Yard. Transcending the field of familiarity of the administration, you are endangering its authority and casting a blow at its self-confidence. The way the threat is handled is by a continual and standardized underrating of the children: They can't do it, couldn't do it, wouldn't like it, don't deserve it . . . In such a manner, many children are tragically and unjustifiably held back from a great many of the good things that they might come to like or admire and are pinned down instead to books the teacher knows and to easy tastes that she can handle. This includes, above all, of course, the kind of material that is contained in the Course of Study.

Try to imagine, for a child, how great the gap between the outside world and the world conveyed within this kind of school must seem: A little girl, maybe Negro, comes in from a street that is lined with car-carcasses. Old purple Hudsons and one-wheel-missing Cadillacs represent her horizon and mark the edges of her dreams. In the kitchen of her house roaches creep and large rats crawl. On the way to school a wino totters. Some teenage white boys slow down their car to insult her, and speed on. At school, she stands frozen for fifteen minutes in a yard of cracked cement that overlooks a hillside on which trash has been unloaded and at the bottom of which the New York, New Haven and Hartford Railroad rumbles past. In the basement, she sits upon broken or splintery seats in filthy toilets and

she is yelled at in the halls. Upstairs, when something has been stolen, she is told that she is the
one who stole it and is called a liar and forced ab-
jectly to apologize before a teacher who has not
the slightest idea in the world of who the culprit
truly was. The same teacher, behind the child's back,
ponders audibly with imagined compassion: "What
can you do with this kind of material? How can
you begin to teach this kind of child?"

Gradually going crazy, the child is sent after two
years of misery to a pupil adjustment counselor
who arranges for her to have some tests and con-
siders the entire situation and discusses it with the
teacher and finally files a long report. She is, some
months later, put onto a waiting-list some place for
once-a-week therapy but another year passes before
she has gotten anywhere near to the front of a long
line. By now she is fourteen, has lost whatever in-
nocence she still had in the back seat of the old
Cadillac and, within two additional years, she will
be ready and eager for dropping out of school.

Once at school, when she was eight or nine, she
drew a picture of a rich-looking lady in an evening
gown with a handsome man bowing before her but
she was told by an insensate and wild-eyed teacher
that what she had done was junk and garbage and
the picture was torn up and thrown away before
her eyes. The rock and roll music that she hears on
the Negro station is considered "primitive" by her
teachers but she prefers its insistent rhythms to the
dreary monotony of school. Once, in Fourth Grade,
she got excited at school about some writing she had
never heard about before. A handsome green book,
brand new, was held up before her and then put
into her hands. Out of this book her teacher read a
poem. The poem was about a Negro—a woman who
was a maid in the house of a white person—and
she liked it. It remained in her memory. Somehow
without meaning to, she found that she had done
the impossible for her: she had memorized that

poem. Perhaps, horribly, in the heart of her already she was aware that it was telling about her future: fifty dollars a week to scrub floors and bathe little white babies in the suburbs after an hour's street-car ride. The poem made her want to cry. The white lady, the lady for whom the maid was working, told the maid she loved her. But the maid in the poem wasn't going to tell any lies in return. She knew she didn't feel any love for the white lady and she told the lady so. The poem was shocking to her, but it seemed bitter, strong and true. Another poem in the same green book was about a little boy on a merry-go-round. She laughed with the class at the question he asked about a Jim Crow section on a merry-go-round, but she also was old enough to know that it was not a funny poem really and it made her, valuably, sad. She wanted to know how she could get hold of that poem, and maybe that whole book. The poems were moving to her . . .

This was a child in my class. Details are changed somewhat but it is essentially one child. The girl was one of the three unplaced special students in that Fourth Grade room. She was not an easy girl to teach and it was hard even to keep her at her seat on many mornings, but I do not remember that there was any difficulty at all in gaining and holding onto her attention on the day that I brought in that green book of Langston Hughes.

Of all of the poems of Langston Hughes that I read to my Fourth Graders, the one that the children liked most was a poem that has the title "Ballad of the Landlord." The poem is printed along with some other material in the back part of this book. This poem may not satisfy the taste of every critic, and I am not making any claims to immortality for a poem just because I happen to like it a great deal. But the reason this poem did have so much value and meaning for me and, I believe, for many of my students, is that it not only seems moving in an obvious and immediate human way but that it *finds* its emotion in something ordinary. It is a poem which really does allow both heroism and pathos to poor people, sees strength in awkwardness and attributes to a poor person standing on the stoop of his slum house every bit as much significance as William Wordsworth saw in daffodils, waterfalls and clouds. At the request of the children later on I mimeographed that poem and, although nobody in the classroom was asked to do this, several of the children took it home and memorized it on their own. I did not assign it for memory, because I do not think that memorizing a poem has any special value. Some of the children just came in and asked if they could recite it. Before long, almost every child in the room had asked to have a turn.

All of the poems that you read to Negro children obviously are not going to be by or about Negro people. Nor would anyone expect that all poems which are read to a class of poor children ought to be grim or gloomy or heart-breaking or sad. But when, among the works of many different authors, you do have the will to read children a poem by a man so highly renowned as Langston Hughes, then I think it is important not to try to pick a poem that is innocuous, being like any other poet's kind of poem, but I think you ought to choose a poem that is genuinely representative and then try to make it real to the children in front of you in the way that I tried. I also think it ought to be taken seriously by a teacher when a group of young children come in to him one morning and announce that they have liked something so much that they have memorized it voluntarily. It surprised me and impressed me when that happened. It was all I needed to know to confirm for me the value of reading that poem and the value of reading many other poems to children which will build upon, and not attempt to break down, the most important observations and very deepest foundations of their lives.

NINETEEN

ONE morning in the spring, as I was putting work up on the blackboard, the Reading Teacher came into my room to chat with me. There still were a few minutes before the children would come in. It was a bright, cheerful morning and she was in a bright and cheerful mood. Before her, on the table beside my desk, were several piles of new books from the library and piles of mimeographed poetry, including the poems by Frost and Langston Hughes. On the back of the door that led into the room was the chart that gave my class's math and spelling scores. The math grades stopped suddenly at the score of 36, then there was a week's jump to 60, and the grade after that was 79.

Deleted from those averages, however, were the scores of five or six pupils who were so hopelessly behind that it seemed no longer meaningful even to include their average in a final grade since they actually could score no grade at all. Among those children, thus excluded from our final reckonings, was the boy I have called Edward. Edward, that week, was still learning to add nine and three and to subtract six from eight. I also was trying hard to teach him to tell time. Some of the children who were doing well in math would take turns working with him. At moments when some kind of small victory was made, his helper would bring him back up to my desk to show me what he had learned. When I saw how much could be done even in such a short time and in such grimy circumstances, I used to

wonder about the judgment of those who said
that a boy like Edward could not be taught within a
normal room. He was having a hard time still and his
day was a steady stream of disappointments. But
he was learning something. He was learning to tell
time.

While she still stood there, chatting, beside the
doorway, and while I was hurrying to get all the
morning's work up on the board, the Reading
Teacher looked out at the sunshine and she said to
me happily: "Spring is a wonderful season for a
teacher, Johnny." She looked at me, and she added:
"It's a time when all of the hard gains of the year's
work come to view."

I knew what she meant by this and I knew that
it was partly out of habit that she said it. But
partly, once again, I was bothered by the tone of
what she said. It suggested to me that she was una-
ware of too much of the pain and too much of the
waste around us in this school and it was clear from
the sound of her voice that she allowed herself no
sense at all of the extent of the tragedy which this
year had been for many children. A few days before,
I had taken my children to the zoo and Edward,
gazing in wonderment and envy at the monkey in the
cage, had said to me unhesitantly: "I wish I could
be him." The same day a toy snake I had given
him broke in two somehow and he instantly col-
lapsed on the ground and began squirming on his
belly and writhing in pain. He wept and screamed.
At length I bought him another toy snake and he
picked it up in his hand and stopped crying. An
occurrence of that sort seemed characteristic of his
school career. Yet he, like Stephen, like Frederick,
had been receiving regular rattannings down in the
cellar all year long. I wondered if the Reading
Teacher was thinking of him, too, when she told
me that spring was a wonderful season for a teacher.

On a day a week later, about fifteen minutes before lunchtime, I was standing in front of the class and they were listening to a record I had brought in. The record was a collection of French children's songs. We had been spending the month reading and talking about Paris and about France. As lunchtime drew near I decided to let the children listen to the music while they were having their meal. While the record was playing, a little signal on the wall began to buzz. I left the room and hurried to the Principal's office. A white man whom I had never seen before was sitting by the Principal's desk. This man, bristling and clearly hostile to me, as was the Principal, instantly attacked me for having read to my class and distributed at their wish the poem I have talked about that was entitled "Ballad of the Landlord." It turned out that he was the father of one of the white boys in the class. He was also a police officer. The mimeograph of the poem, in my handwriting, was waved before my eyes. The Principal demanded to know what right I had to allow such a poem—not in the official Course of Study—to be read and memorized by the children in my class. I said I had not asked anyone to memorize it but that I would defend the poem and its use against her or anyone on the basis that it was a good poem. The Principal became incensed with my answer and blurted out that she did not consider it a work of art. I remember that I knew right away I was not going to give in to her. I replied, in my own anger, that I had spent a good many years studying poetry and that I was not going to accept her judgment about a poem that meant that much to me and to my pupils. Although I did not say it in these words, it was really a way of telling her that I thought myself a better judge of poetry than she. I hope that I am.

The parent attacked me, as well, for having forced his son to read a book about the United Nations. I had brought a book to class, one out of sixty or more volumes, that told about the U.N. and its Human Rights Commission. The man, I believe, had mistaken "human rights" for "civil rights" and he was consequently in a patriotic rage. The Principal, in fairness, made the point that she did not think there was anything really wrong with the United Nations, although in the report that she later filed on the matter, she denied this for some reason and said, instead, "I then spoke and said that I felt there was no need for this material in the classroom.' The Principal's report goes on to say that, after she dismissed me to my own room, she assured the parent that "there was not another teacher in the district who would have used this poem or any material like it. I assured him that his children would be very safe from such incidents."

As the Principal had instructed, I returned to my class, where the children had remained quiet and had not even opened up their lunch because I had not told them to and they were patiently waiting for me to come back. We had our lunch and listened to more music and did the rest of our lessons and at quarter to two, just before school ended, the Principal called me back again. She told me I was fired. This was about eight days before the end of school. I asked her whether this was due to the talk we had had earlier but she said it was not. I asked her if it was due to an evaluation, a written report, which I had sent in on the compensatory program about a week before. This was a report that I had written, as all teachers had, in answer to a request from the School Department and in which I had said that the program seemed to me to be very poor. I was told, at the time I passed it in, that the Principal had been quite angry. But again she said it was not that. I asked her finally if my dismissal was at her request and she said, No, it came from higher up and she didn't know anything about it except that I should close up my records and leave school and not come back. She said that I should not say good-bye to the children in my class. I asked her if she really meant this and she repeated it to me as an order.

I returned to my class, taught for ten more minutes, then gave assignments for the following morning as if I would be there and saw the children file off. After all but one were gone, that one, a little girl, helped me to pile up the books and posters and pictures with which I had tried to fill the room. It took an hour to get everything out and when it was all in my car it filled up the back seat and the space behind it and the floor, as well as the floor and half the seat in front. Outside my car, on the sidewalk, I said good-bye to this one child and told her that I would not be back again. I told her I had had a disagreement with the Principal and I asked her to say good-bye to the other children. I regretted very much now that I had not disobeyed the Principal's last order and I wished that I could have had one final chance to speak to all my pupils. The little girl, in any case, took what I had said with great solemnity and promised that she would relay my message to the other children. Then I left the school.

The next morning, an official who had charge of my case at the School Department contradicted the Principal by telling me that I was being fired at her wish. The woman to whom I spoke said the reason was the use of the poem by Langston Hughes, which was punishable because it was not in the Course of Study. She also said something to me at the time that had never been said to me before, and something that represented a much harder line on curriculum innovation than I had ever seen in print. No literature, she said, which is not in the Course of Study can *ever* be read by a Boston teacher without permission from someone higher up. When I asked her about this in more detail, she said further that no poem anyway by any Negro author can be considered permissible if it involves suffering. I thought this a very strong statement and I asked her several times again if that was really what she meant. She insisted that it was.

I asked if there would be many good poems left to read by such a standard. Wouldn't it rule out almost all great Negro literature? Her answer evaded the issue. No poetry that described suffering was felt to be suitable. The only Negro poetry that could be read in the Boston schools, she indicated, must fit a certain kind of standard or canon. The kind of poem she meant, she said by example, might be a poem that "accentuates the positive" or "describes nature" or "tells of something hopeful." Nothing was wanted of suffering, nothing that could be painful, nothing that might involve its reader in a moment of self-questioning or worry. If this is an extremely conservative or eccentric viewpoint, I think that it is nonetheless something which has to be taken seriously. For an opinion put forward in the privacy of her office by a School Department official who has the kind of authority that that woman had must be taken to represent a certain segment of educational opinion within the Boston school system and in some ways it seems more representative even than the carefully written and carefully prepared essays of such a lady as the Deputy Superintendent. For in those various writings Miss Sullivan unquestionably has had one ear tuned to the way they were going to come across in print and sound in public whereas, in the office of a central bureaucratic person such as the lady with whom I now was talking, you receive an absolutely innocent and unedited experience in what a school system really feels and believes.

The same official went on a few minutes later to tell me that, in addition to having made the mistake of reading the wrong poem, I also had made an error by bringing in books to school from the Cambridge Public Library. When I told her that there were no books for reading in our classroom, except for the sets of antiquated readers, and that the need of the children was for individual reading which they would be able to begin without delay, she told me that that was all very well but still this was the Boston school system and that meant that you must not use a book that the Cambridge Library supplied. She also advised me, in answer to my question, that any complaint from a parent means automatic dismissal of a teacher anyway and that this, in itself, was therefore sufficient grounds for my release. When I repeated this later to some Negro parents they were embittered and startled. For they told me of many instances in which they had complained that a teacher whipped their child black and blue or called him a nigger openly and yet the teacher had not been released. It seemed obvious to them, as it seems to me, and would to anyone, that a complaint from a white police officer carries more weight in the Boston school system than the complaint of the mother of a Negro child.

I asked this official finally whether I had been considered a good teacher and what rating I had been given. She answered that she was not allowed to tell me. An instant later, whimsically reversing herself, she opened her files and told me that my rating was good. The last thing she said was that deviation from a prescribed curriculum was a serious offense and that I would never be permitted to teach in Boston again. The words she used were these: "You're out. You cannot teach in the Boston schools again. If you want to teach why don't you try a private school someday." I left her office but, before I left the building, I stopped at a table and I took out a pad of paper and wrote down what she had said.

The firing of a "provisional teacher" from a large public school system is not generally much of an event. As Mr. Ohrenberger was to say later, it happens commonly. When the firing is attributed to

something as socially relevant and dramatically specific as a single poem by a well-known Negro poet,
however, it is not apt to go unnoticed; and, in this
case, I was not ready to let it go unnoticed. I tele-
phoned one of the civil rights leaders of Roxbury and
told him what had happened. He urged me to call
Phyllis Ryan, press spokesman for the Boston chapter
of CORE. Mrs. Ryan decided to set up a press conference for the same day. That afternoon, sitting
at the side of the Negro minister who had begun
and carried on a lonely vigil for so many days outside the Boston School Committee, I described what
had just happened.

The reaction of the reporters seemed, for the most
part, as astonished as my own, and the direct consequence of this was that Miss Sullivan and Mr.
Ohrenberger were obliged in a hurry, and without
checking carefully, to back up the assertions of their
own subordinates. The consequence of this, in turn,
was that both of them allowed themselves to repeat
and to magnify misstatements. Mr. Ohrenberger came
out with a statement that I had been "repeatedly
warned" about deviation from the Course of Study.
Miss Sullivan's statement on my dismissal was much
the same as Mr. Ohrenberger's, adding, however, a
general admonition about the dangers of reading to
Negro children poems written in bad grammar. Although Langston Hughes "has written much beautiful poetry," she said, "we cannot give directives to
the teachers to use literature written in native dia-
lects." It was at this time that she also made the
statement to which I have alluded earlier: "We are
trying to break the speech patterns of these children,
trying to get them to speak properly. This poem does
not present correct grammatical expression and
would just entrench the speech patterns we want to
break." I felt it was a grim statement.

The reactions of a large number of private individuals were recounted in the press during the fol-

lowing weeks, and some of them gave me a better feeling about the city in which I grew up than I had ever had before. One school employee who asked, for his safety, to remain anonymous, gave a statement to the press in which he reported that the atmosphere at school on the civil rights subject was like the atmosphere of a Gestapo. I believe that the person in question was a teacher in my school, but the fact that he had felt it necessary to keep his name anonymous, and his position unspecified, made his statement even more revelatory than if his name and position had appeared.

Another thing that reassured me was the reaction of the parents of the children in my class and in the school. I did not have any means of contacting them directly, but dozens of CORE members went out into the neighborhood, knocked at doors, and told parents very simply that a teacher had been fired for reading their children a good poem written by a Negro. A meeting was called by the chairman of the parent group, a woman of great poise and courage, and the parents asked me if I would come to that meeting and describe for them what had gone on. I arrived at it late and I was reluctant to go inside but, when I did go in, I found one of the most impressive parent groups that I had ever seen gathered in one hall. Instead of ten or eleven or twelve or fifteen or even twenty or thirty, which was the number of parents that usually could be rallied for a meeting on any ordinary occasion during the year, there were in the church building close to two hundred people and I discovered that several of my pupils were in the audience as well as over half the parents of the children in my class.

I do not want to describe all the things that were said that night, what statements of strong loyalty came forward from those mothers and fathers, or how they developed, step by step, the plan of protest which they would put into effect on the following morning and which was to be the subject of intensive press attention for a good many days to come. Looking back on it, I am sure that it was one of the most important and most valuable and most straightforward moments in my life. A white woman who was present, and who has observed race relations in Roxbury for a long while, said to me after the meeting: "I hope that you understand what happened tonight between you and those parents. Very few white people in all of their lives are ever going to be given that kind of tribute. You can do anything in your life—and I don't know what plans you have. But you will never have a better reason to feel proud."

I believed that what she said was true. It is hard to imagine that any other event in my life can matter more.

In the days after that meeting, there were a number of demonstrations at the school which had a disruptive effect on certain classes. Whether this is a good thing or a bad thing, many people may not be sure. The question is whether it is a real loss to miss one or two or even three or four days of school when none of the days that you are spending in school is worth much anyway. The Art and Reading Teachers, as well as many of the other older teachers, I was told, went on teaching and talking and grading as if in total oblivion of the turmoil breaking all around them and as if they had no idea that anything out of the ordinary might be going on. On the Monday after my firing, the parents of many students in my class kept their children home from school and went up to sit all day at their children's desks themselves. This action brought the Deputy Superintendent to the school building, and she cajoled and pleaded with the parents to give up their protest but, for once perhaps in her career, diplomacy of that type just did not work. Although the parents consented at last to leave the building at her request, they did not give up the demonstration and they returned to the school two days later to carry out a longer and larger protest. At length, it took a member of the School Committee, Mr. Eisenstadt, to persuade the parents to give up their sit-in at the school. He achieved this purpose by promising them a thorough investigation into the entire matter. Before he began the investigation, however, he told me on the telephone and he told the press as well that he felt the firing was completely justified. His announcement of such a pre-judgment, along with his expressed intention to investigate anyway, seemed to me to place him in an ambiguous position and I did not therefore expect a great deal from the investigation he now was about to undertake.

TWENTY

ONE night, about a week after my dismissal, I decided to call the Reading Teacher on the phone. Despite my dislike for certain things she did and things she told me, I still had been closer to her than to any other person during most of the year, and closer really than I had been to either the Art or Math Teacher. For this reason I called her but I did not have a pleasant conversation with her and, because of the things it brought out about her feelings, I regretted afterward that I had made the call at all.

Her manner to me was icy from the beginning and, before many moments had passed, I began to understand why. She felt that my dismissal, and the publicity that had attended it, had put the whole school under a spotlight and she felt that this had invaded her privacy and compromised her way of doing things. The very idea of disruption was anathema to her, and the fact that in this case the disruption had come so near and had actually brought the parents of the children, and with them the outside world, into the schoolhouse, seemed to her horrifying. She spoke of the invading parents with vivid disgust and with repulsion:

"They threatened us! They told us they would go to the toilet right there on the floor if we wouldn't let them use the bathrooms!"

This, she flung at me as if it were living proof of the essential barbarism of all Negro parents: a barbarism, of course, of which she had been fully convinced from the beginning and for which she had never really needed confirmation. The longer we spoke, the more apparent it became that her resentment and her sense of condemnation toward me were eating her alive and that they were beginning to take on the dimensions of a moral rage. Her viewpoint on the events that had transpired, and on the way in which I had conducted myself, came down ultimately to two dominant concerns. One was the way in which these events and my words of comment upon them might in some drastic way have affected her career. The other was the way in which the same events might have affected the security and peace of mind of some of the white children in the school. Of the Negro children, of the community, of the people whose boys and girls made up the vast majority of the student body, she had not a friendly word to say. Her only observation about the children was that those who had joined the picket line were now "surly" and "insolent" and had given the teachers a dreadful time in school.

Her concern for the way in which all of this affected the white children was obviously foremost in her mind. She went on to assert, for example, that several of the white children were now being picked on and teased and taunted a great deal. "How does poor Susan deserve it?" she asked me. "Do you feel no sympathy for Roger or for Ellen?" Hearing her talk, one might easily have believed that I had just driven in a new and previously unknown wedge between the races. It was as if I had created or elicited, single-handed, a wave of formerly non-existent animosity and distrust. She expressed her feelings in these words: "Do you remember what I said to you about the Negro funeral? Do you remember when I described to you how primitive and emotional it was? It is that same primitive emotion which we are seeing now."

This did not seem a more disheartening statement

than the words she had spoken about the Negro
parents. It came of a similar aversion and was born
of the same offended mind. Of the Negro children
who had been my students, she made only one additional remark. Of all the children I had taught, she
said, of all the Fourth Grade children who had been
in either class, naturally the first one to go out and
join the picket line was Angelina: the one little
girl whose talent she had so passionately underrated
and whose possibilities, whether as a painter or just
as a unique and live-wire little person, she had done
her best to ignore. This child, she now told me, had
joined the picket line to protest my firing and subsequently had grown more insolent than she had ever
been before. As it happened, although there were
many children out walking on the picket line, I did
not ever see Angelina there. But I do remember
thinking that, if it was really so, then it surely was
no wonder that a little girl might well be insolent
and surly to a teacher who had never respected her.
Angelina was one of a number of children of whom
the Reading Teacher had frequently told me she was
being "insolent," and it was something that I could
never understand. The only thing she had ever done
with me that could have been called "insolent" was
to treat me naturally as a human being and to kid
with me a little on my own grounds, or at other
times, like any normal child, to let her attention
wander off. Sometimes I punished her in a mild way
when I thought she was getting kind of jumpy, although God knows that jumpiness is hardly the worst
crime in the world and, in a school system like Boston's, it sometimes seems a kind of virtue. The truth
is that I was always astonished when the Reading
Teacher told me of an insolence or surliness in the
child which I could have sworn was never there.

A few days after that, I spoke on the phone to
another teacher in my school. She told me that, immediately after my firing, the Reading Teacher had

warned her against speaking too much of the truth about the school. I was told by another Boston teacher, who taught in a different school, that the older instructors in his school had reacted in a manner that was very much the same.

"If this young man is right—if all of these younger people are right—if the educational scholars are right—if the new State Report is right—if the civil rights leaders are right—if Martin Luther King is right—then we are not merely in some error which may perhaps have to be somehow corrected but, rather—and far more inexorable and terrible—our entire view of the world has just been shattered and our entire lives may have been a waste."

This was essentially the substance of what they are saying, and the Reading Teacher had spoken to me in that manner, if not in those words, on many occasions during the school year. Only once during that year do I remember a brief moment when, for an instant, the terrible doubt and delicate balance involved in that intricate structure of defense became apparent to her and began to totter. There was a day when we were talking and when we came suddenly to a point of unexpected agreement about the miserable consequences, for teacher and children alike, of being within this kind of school. At that moment, instinctively, when for an instant I felt convinced that she was ready to agree with me, she drew herself back suddenly, halted in her progress, as it were, and said to me hurriedly: "No. My life is set." I remember feeling pity and embarrassment. The feeling I had was that I had done something unkind to her by getting my own soul out of prison, and it was as if in effect, by ceasing to hedge my own words, I had begun to confiscate something that she needed badly. But also and at the same time I remember feeling a sense of disappointment and regret that I had never gone at all far enough in that direction of honesty and I also felt a wave of self-accusation that I had not been talking to her and to many of the other teachers in that manner all year long.

Today, I am convinced that the second feeling was the only right one, and my greatest regret out of a school year filled with many disappointments is the single disappointment over my excessive concern with the feelings of a few teachers and the related disappointment that I could not consistently have placed the claims of several hundred children above the private egotism of a handful of adults. Miss Sullivan may have been right when she spoke, as she did often, about her "dedicated teachers." But if they were dedicated, then what many were dedicated to above all was the extension of their own personalities and the perpetuation of their own code of values in the hearts and minds of children. You do not get something for nothing, I am afraid, and I do not really think we are ever going to get a good school posed by the veteran teachers of that sort. All the system until we can deal effectively with the problem fables in the world of how dedicated and devoted they are cannot change this single overriding fact.

In the weeks following my dismissal Mr. Eisenstadt held interviews with me and with two or three other teachers and let it be understood that he was conducting an investigation. He told me, however, that few of the teachers in my school were willing to speak up. Only one teacher came forward to speak in my behalf, and I am under the impression that Mr. Eisenstadt did not find her testimony credible for he discounted it. At length he issued his report. Far from exonerating me, he attacked me and condemned me quite severely, more severely in fact than I had been attacked before. "It should be understood," he wrote, "that many temporary teachers are released from service every year by the administration of the Boston Public Schools. They are released for a variety of reasons. The overwhelming majority of such cases are discharged because in the opinion of the administrators and supervisors the certain temporary teachers are found unsuitable in training, personality, or character. Mr. Kozol, or anyone else who lacks the personal discipline to abide by rules and regulations, as we all must in our civilized society, is obviously unsuited for the highly responsible profession of teaching."

No longer being allowed to work in Boston as a teacher, I spent the next year running a tutorial center in Roxbury. Since then, wanting to be a teacher again, I applied to some of the public school systems of the outlying suburbs. I accepted a good position finally in the public schools of Newton, although the gratitude and sense of excitement that I felt were also complicated and mixed with other feelings. For the position I was given placed me in the company of some fine teachers and under the supervision of a distinguished principal and also, and above all, of course it put me back in a classroom again and gave me the chance to work with children. But at the same time it took me away from the one place where I had the deepest involvement and from the one place where I would really have wanted most to be. Since those days, nevertheless, I have moved to Roxbury, where I live today, and I have been able to keep in touch with a number of the mothers and fathers of the pupils in my former school. I also have kept in touch with several of the children.

Three whom I have not seen, however, are Frederick and Edward and Stephen. The reason for this is that all three of these boys, who had been my Fourth Grade students, were gotten out of the public school system in Boston almost at the same time as I. Edward, I am told, went into a private class for disturbed children. Stephen went into a home for the emotionally disturbed. Frederick, the following autumn, was sent away to a child's reformatory run

by the State of Massachusetts. I do not believe that
an institution would have been necessary for any
of those boys if they had ever received anything
like humane education and respect from anything
like enlightened teachers within anything like a decent school. Those are the three children to whom
I felt closest while I was in the school system. The
fact that they have been served so poorly by public
education does not seem forgivable.

In the fall of 1965 the School Committee election
returned to power all four bigots on the Boston
School Committee. Mr. Eisenstadt ran up an easy victory next in line after Mrs. Hicks. Mr. Gartland, the
one man who had been a friend to education and
a friend to Negro people, was defeated and replaced
in fifth position by a previously unknown politician
who espoused some of the views of Mrs. Hicks. In
the time since that election, there has been an in-
creasing growth of black nationalism in the Roxbury
ghetto and the Negro leadership has been speaking
for the first time of withdrawing from the City of
Boston and of establishing its own Negro institutions.
It is not difficult to understand why this would seem
desirable, and it is very hard for someone who lives
among the Negro people to argue against it, much
as he might consider it unwise.

DOCUMENTS

RACIAL RATIOS

[This is the speech delivered by Joseph Lee before the Boston School Committee on Wednesday, March 3, 1965.]

THE heed of the Boston public schools for 100 years has been to promote the Negro pupil into the adult world as a full participant in American life, both as to his supplying products for earned payment and in procuring purchases for his prosperity.

There are those who think that this could be expedited if no school building were allowed in which Negro pupils were a majority, and if, in every school building, Negroes were a minority.

The Boston School Committee at no time has been averse to such a racial ratio. Faith in a busy and rewarded future, general to pupils of another race, might become more general to Negro children, if they attended classes where pupils of other race were in the majority.

Until the recent influx of Negroes from the South, indeed, Negroes in Boston always attended schools where they were in the racial minority.

A few years ago, Boston Negroes were settled on the out-of-town slope of Beacon Hill—where they were welcomed into predominantly white schools.

Of late, they have moved to the low rental areas of Roxbury—where they were welcomed into predominantly white schools. But they still encountered difficulty in meeting a future as replete as the average white citizen's.

With the arrival of triple numbers still later from the South, Negro residents have spread out in their settlements, into the South End, Dorchester, Jamaica Plain, and farther districts, where they were again welcomed into schools predominantly white.

Now, most congested in Roxbury and the South End,

they attend schools there, where it is now they who make up a majority.

It is notable that they were repelled from the soil of the suburbs partly upon the pre-emption of those lands by more prosperous purchasers of other races, and partly by the harsh or underhanded denial to them of those tracts by landowners rigging the market against America.

Suppose now the School Committee wishes again to have no school in which the majority is made of Negro pupils, and have only schools in which the majority is made of white pupils.

Or suppose some powerful order goes out with ruling force, to compel the School Committee to that proportionment.

By what plan will the School Committee then proceed? What will we run into? What will it amount to?

First, the schools in the Negro heartland of Boston will have to be broken up. Otherwise racial re-assortment will not be accomplished. A single school, or half a school, left in the Negro core-land would be almost exclusively Negro.

It will not do, *second*, to dabble in half-measures at the fringe of the Negro residential territory. Schools around the edge are mixed already with a majority of Nordic and pale-faced children, eggshell-colored—whose "treacherous blood betrays with blushing the close enacts and counsels of their hearts."

To move the Negro majority at the core out into schools on the rim would merely transplant the Negro majority farther out. It is like the mark on the knee of a child's breeches when he falls on a tarry schoolyard or street. The cleansing fluid will relieve the mark all right. But the mark will just reappear as a ring on the cloth at the outermost reaches of the cleansing fluid.

The Negro majority of the interior will merely appear as a Negro majority around the exterior, defeating the purpose (shifting the geography, that is, but retaining the same Negro majority).

Besides, the white parents prefer schools preponderantly white for their children—the same white majority that the Negro leaders prefer. If the Negro density at the Negro residential core is pushed farther out to form Negro majorities in schools at the rim, white families will retreat and retreat.

Already 100,000 people have left Boston for the suburbs.

Moreover, Negro mothers have twice the birthrate of white mothers. With this, plus the arrival of new Negro families every day from the South, the frontier of Negro pupils, sent from their residential core out into schools on the fringe, will advance outward and outward: and costly schools built this year will be abandoned next year, as the frontier expands.

No; the Negro pupils at the core will have to leapfrog over the already racially mixed schools at the fringe and settle in out-lying schools now mostly all white—to avoid an aggravated packing of Negro pupils in the borderline schools.

Such a leapfrogging of Negro pupils at the center out to nearly all-white schools on the outskirts, if evenly distributed, would, indeed, accomplish the desired white majority and Negro minority in every classroom.

But now a flaw looms.

Lo, the Interim Report of the Advisory Committee on Racial Imbalance in Education, of the Massachusetts State Board of Education, in a welter of conflicting opinions, seems to say that the ideal Negro minority is just under 4%. This is the ratio of Negro school children to white in the Commonwealth. And 4% means 1 out of 25. A single Negro child to every classroom of 25 children! This is the optimum proportion of Negro pupils to white pupils obtainable in Massachusetts.

But if Boston, instead, distributed Negroes in accord with the proportion of Negro children to white children prevailing within the confines of Boston, then Boston, with more than 20% of its pupils Negro, would have 5 or 6 Negro pupils in every classroom.

And this would bring the wrath of the suburbs, who repel Negroes and harbor a much smaller ratio of Negroes in their population than the State average—in fact, only 1% of Negroes, just 1 to every 4 suburban

classrooms—it would bring suburban contempt down
upon the head of Boston, which has 20% of its pupils
Negro. And they would brand Boston as one vast Negro
ghetto. In the eyes of these report-makers, Boston has
committed the wrong of opening its arms to Negroes
to the extent of 20 times as many Negroes in proportion to its population as the immediate suburbs, and
6 times as many as the State average. An even distribution of Boston Negroes in every Boston classroom
does not relieve that. Something more needs to be done
in avoiding Negro localization upon the land of Boston.

To rid the situation of emotionalism, let us fall in
with those critics who say that the majority of the
present Boston School Committee consists of bigots and
race supremacists. [They do—from audience.] If that
be so, the Boston School Committee would be the first
to wish a 4 to 1 majority of white children in every
classroom. That would accord with the overall 4 to 1
predominance of white children in Boston. And it would
make a huge white ascendancy in every school. And, if
really racially biased, the Boston School Committee,
even more, would desire a 24 to 1 preponderance of
white children to Negroes in every classroom. That would
accord with the 24 to 1 ratio of whites to Negroes
throughout the Commonwealth idealized by the State
Commission's report. And it would make an overwhelming predominance of white children in every classroom.
Still more particularly, the very last thing that an im-
putedly prejudiced Boston School Committee would desire would be the status quo, where in many classrooms
it is the white children who are only 5 among 20 Negro
children, and sometimes a minority of only 1 among 24
Negro pupils. Any white racist would abhor the present
situation and would immediately want to change it, so
that white pupils would no longer be submerged by
Negro majorities in 45 Boston schools.

So, the School Committee, whatever its wrong-minded-
ness or right-mindedness, in no case can object to the
Negro spokesmen's demand for a distribution of Negro

pupils in its schools along the ideal plan of a 4-to-1 outnumbering by white children over Negro children, according to Boston's utmost possibilities, or an even more ideal 24-to-1 outnumbering by white children over Negro children, according to the State Commission's maximum combination for the Commonwealth.

But, again, how to get it.

Well, *third*, to achieve such ratios, the School Committee must use force.

Left with a choice, Negro parents do not wish their Elementary School children dispersed to other schools, far from home.

There have been several tests and trials of this.

When one school grade, made up of mostly Negro children, was moved from a building on St. Botolph Street a few blocks away to a mostly white school on Newbury Street, the Negro parents unanimously petitioned the School Committee at the end of the school year to have their children back in the mainly Negro school by the next year. It is human to want to be in the majority.

Under our Open Enrollment Policy also, which lets parents send their children to any school in the city not pre-occupied by its neighborhood children, it has been mostly the white children who have taken advantage of such latitude. Few Negro children have.

With no cost of transportation, too, the Negro children of the inner South End have not taken the 20-minute walk of one mile to the 300 empty seats in the Peter Faneuil School on Beacon Hill, even though 20 minutes is not a long time to spend going to school, and the walk across Boston Common up past the glories of the State House—past the immortal statue of America's Negro heroes—is robust and rewarding.

And when parents recently answered a questionaire offering transportation of their children from overcrowded schools in Dorchester not far from Franklin Park, to outlying schools mainly white farther from town, only 11% of the total Negro and white parents of children in those crowded and approximately 66%

Negro-occupied schools voted affirmatively to accept the offered transfer by bus.

And, for finality, a recent Louis Harris poll of Negroes across the nation tells us that the majority of Negroes are now opposed to the carrying of their school children to other neighborhoods.

To overcome the reluctance of Negro parents to disperse their Elementary School children to schools at a distance, compulsion would be necessary.

And then the protest! Discrimination would be charged.

Negro parents would say: "If the white children can go to school around the corner from their homes, why can't we Negroes? Can't we have any schools in our neighborhood? Why must Negro children walk past the closed neighborhood school next door to catch a bus at a pickup point at a particular instant and be whisked miles away from their homes? Are we Negroes second-class citizens?"

You can push human nature just so far.

Fourth, our Open Enrollment Policy would have to be given up. Otherwise, as soon as a Negro child was hauled to his new school outside his area, he would petition to come back—and could not be refused unless our Open Enrollment Policy had been repealed in favor of authoritarian pupil assignments.

Fifth, the Negro elementary school pupil, recently come from the South, if shifted to a mainly white school away from his home, would have to forfeit the special education now established (for his needs) in most of his neighborhood schools at the request of the National Association for the Advancement of Colored People. Such instruction is designed to bridge the gap between such Negro children's cultural background and the northern society into which they are going. These courses impose a 25% greater cost for a Negro child's education on Boston than a white child's. (The Negro child would lose this, if shifted to a mainly white school. Such courses in a school predominantly white do not exist, and would be useless, retardatory, and irrelevant, if they did.)

In this differentiation between certain Negro children and the majority of white children, the matter is not one of racial difference. Within the year the Mayor of Beersheba addressed the Mayor, City Council, and School Committee of Boston, to describe the growth of his ancient wilderness to a city of 50,000 people. He chose to reveal his chief municipal woe as having to go beyond the ease of educating Jewish children arriving to enter his schools from Czechoslovakia, France, and Poland, with a vocabulary of many words and a good command of sentence structure, and having to take on the staggering difficulty of trying to educate Jewish children coming from unprosperous North Africa and the Arabian peninsula, with only a small headful of words, and in command of sentences no more than five words long, and with little faith in learning. Here there is no distinction of race against race, but only prosperous Jews against unprosperous Jews. In Boston, the same divergence comes up between the children of unprospering Negro families, who *do* need and get the tailor-made and costly instruction, and the children of prospering Negro families, together with prospering white families, who do not get it. (Boston's unprospering Negro children, then, would have to give up this special instruction now furnished in most of their local neighborhood elementary schools, if they transferred to mainly white schools or to Negro schools in prospering districts where such instruction would be superfluous and doesn't exist.)

Sixth, a great many new schools would have to be built in the comparatively prospering, white residential sections of the city, if the 13,000 Negro children who are now in 45 preponderantly Negro schools were transferred from their present neighborhood schools thither. About 35 new schools would have to be built. Presently vacant seats in outlying white schools are not numerically sufficient.

Seventh, a problem in logistics would arise in transporting Negro children from pickup points in their neighborhood to some 115 elementary schools elsewhere in the city. Some 260 buses would be required. At the usual transportational cost of $1 per pupil per day for 180 days, the cost of hauling some 13,000 Negro children from their present predominantly Negro schools to others farther away would be considerable—something near 2½ million dollars a year.

And, *eighth,* resentment might here arise between those Negro children transported to mainly white schools in one part of the city and those Negro children transported to white schools in another part. Boston residents near the outskirts of the city have some of the arrogance and unfairness towards Negroes which the suburbs outside the city show. Negro children transported toward less cordial outposts would wonder why they could not attend school in the more cordial mainland of the city.

Ninth, even if these adversities were all overcome, still the accomplishment of a Negro minority evenly distributed in every Boston classroom would, before long, turn to dust in our hand.

Populations change.

In other words, if the white population of America is to stay about the same, and the Negro population is to double with each generation under its high birthrate, than the *10* Negro units in every present 100 units of American population will become *20* Negro units with the next generation 20 years from now; then it will become *40* Negro units in the second generation 40 years from now; in the third generation *80* units 60 years from now; and *160* units 80 years from now—while the white population remains static at 90 units—so that, if Mr. Eisenstadt lives to a good old age, he will see America a predominantly Negro nation, like Africa.

That Negro-Americans do produce more than twice as many children per mother as do white Americans can be seen from the fact that the Negro pupil is 1 out of 6 Boston pupils (parochial schools included). But the Negro adult is only 1 out of 14 adults in Boston. (Negro children and adults, combined, average-up to 1 Negro out of every 10 persons in the city.) Negro children form more than twice as big a part of the

Negro population as white children form of the white population.

In any case, the population take-over by Negroes will come much sooner in the big warm-hearted cities like Boston than in the cold-blooded suburbs which repel them. In the great northern city of Chicago already—let alone Detroit and Philadelphia—Negroes are more than 50% of the elementary school population. When Negroes become more than 50% of the Boston school population, it is hard to see how the races can be distributed in the classrooms so that the Negroes will always be a minority. The report-makers will then say that the Boston Schools are racially "imbalanced"—every classroom predominantly Negro.

Only recently was today's overwhelmingly Negro Roxbury hitched to Boston. Many people now living can remember Roxbury as a small country town, under its own selectmen, connected to Boston by a narrow isthmus. Its sister town of Brookline was never absorbed. Brookline stuck in Boston's throat geographically, like a red apple in the jaws of a roasted pig. Suppose Roxbury had never been engrossed into Boston. It would then have its own Negro government, its Negro police force, its own schools—to its own liking. Would it then accuse itself of racial discrimination? any more than the all-Negro schools of the new Negro nations of Africa? or the all-Negro and Negro-governed towns in the South and Southwest? Or would it be so accused by others? Is the accident of political jurisdiction, or inclusion in a larger municipality, the matter of irritation? Roxbury is separated from part of Boston by part of the Atlantic ocean, with no bridge between. Roxbury is separated from Brookline by only the Muddy River, with many bridges between. Is it realistic to make past political gerrymandering the determining factor in fuming at Boston's racial life but not at Brookline's? Our Negro families might have made total settlement, not in Roxbury, but in Somerville—equally contiguous but outside Boston's jurisdiction. What then? What if Roxbury had been annexed to Brookline instead of Boston? Anyway, what do you do about maintaining

Negroes in the racial minority in every schoolroom, when a small town or a big city becomes preponderantly Negro in population, as the nation itself changes its racial complexion.

The immediate expense of hauling school children around by bus to different schools in Boston need not be too bothersome. The prodigal public of Boston, through its taxes, now spends more money paying people to live in idleness and to render no requested service to the world than it pays to Boston's 3,000 teachers to strain their souls wrestling Boston's 95,000 school children into prosperous adult life. In other words, more taxpayers' money goes through the so-called "Welfare Department," to unpatronized people whom nobody else will pay, than goes through the Boston School Committee to pay our enlisted and striving teachers. If some of the recipients of Boston's merciful dole strive resolutely to drop it and to offer a week's work for a week's pay, some among them are cruelly rejected because of color, though well qualified, and others only half try, if at all.

A fraction of Boston girls bear children one after another, sired by stray men who don't stay around—with an increase of pay from public alms for every new child. A Gallup survey of New York shows that approximately ⅔ of the 1,000 children born to persons on relief every month enter this world without the benefit of marriage between their parents. The Boston percentage is probably not much less. It does not help a girl to be honorable to pay her with public funds to be the reverse. Disbursements by taxedly charitable Boston to mothers for no-marriage-bells children already are 3 million dollars a year. (And how are our schools to supply a needed father-image in teaching such half-homed and half-backed children?)

However that may figure, it would be just as well to take at least 2½ million dollars out of the 58 million gracious dollars proposed in Boston this year as poor relief to persons who give no service in return, and to pay it, rather, to those among their patient number who are able and willing to go to work driving busses to transport pupils in mostly Negro schools to schools mostly white elsewhere in the city.

If lack of any urgency for such frugal switching of public funds is argued on the grounds that some of our mercy-dollars for local indigents come bountifully from Washington, it may be rejoined that if the earnings of Boston citizens weren't pilfered by the long arm of Washington tax-collectors in the first place, we could use those same tax dollars for poor relief or alternative purposes ourselves much better right here, from the start.

As to the morality of re-allocating tax-raised funds (which, otherwise, are creating a permanent leisure class—lolling in idleness on the backs of the toiling masses—out of both whites and Negroes such as take for granted a continual tax-furnished dole as a way of life) it is argued sometimes as a special condonement for dependence on public aid by occasional Negro-Americans up from the South, here among them, that such Negro-Americans are justly resentful and excusable victims of the ravages and immorality of past slavery. This is important for white citizens to remember. As for matrimony, Negro marriages were seldom allowed under Southern slavery, and unmarried motherhood was the imposed and accepted code. The unconsenting and unrequited Negro girl, too, served the immoral white man's pleasure. It is no worse for the Negro to flout the whole white race because of some bad experiences in the past than for a white man to decry the whole Negro race because of some poor samples.

Yet, for actuality, no young or old Negro-American today has been a slave. Besides, almost the whole population of Boston is made up of persons of Irish, Italian, Polish, Canadian, and Jewish background, who were miles away from America at the time of slavery. If a few Yankees still live in Boston, their grandsires atoned for the sins of their race by shedding their blood in the 4-year horror of Civil War battlefields. Greater love hath no man than this, that he lay down his life for his friends. These battlefields, indeed, were shared by many free Negroes—180,000 Negro soldiers on the Northern side all together. Every inhabitant of Boston should read the back of the Shaw monument once a year. When the North was swept by a demand for the recovery of Colonel Shaw's body from the common trench at Fort Wagner on the northernmost spit of the South Carolina sea islands into which it was flung, his father declared that he would have no part of that, since he knew of no finer monument to be over his son than the piled bodies of Negro soldiers who fell at his side. How much further can you go than that? Every American—Negro-American or otherwise—can and should live on the lessons of the past. No one should live within the past. It is no good to duck the lively present for a dead past.

But even if the cost of bus transportation were met by monies justifiably shifted and re-allocated from other and pudgy public accounts, we would still not be overcoming baleful drawbacks, noted heretofore, like that distasteful compulsion needed to force Negro pupils into distant schools, or that loss of the special education for recently arrived Negroes which they would lose if shifted to white schools—and so forth.

To circumvent all such human and logistical difficulties, the School Committee might offer carfare to a school of his own choice at public expense, for any desirous elementary school pupil, on the public transportation system. This would by no means bring an effective or systematic distribution of Negro children to form perfect and even minorities all around in schools predominantly white. At an estimate, parents of less than 1,000 children, light or dark—mostly 9 years old, 10 years old, or 11 years old, in the upper three grades of elementary school—would find the will or the advantage to have their children so travel. But at least the expense would be minimal. And it would ease a free choice for anyone. The School Committee need not overlook such a possibility.

Further, Junior High Schools, which are few in number and each large in student body, and sparsely scattered over the city, could in the near future be retained or erected only in predominantly white residential areas of the city. Most of them are in such areas now. The same for High Schools.

Yet, for Elementary Schools, confronted with educational losses in taking Negro children away from their present neighborhood schools (with their tailor-made, special instruction) and sobered by the indignity and discrimination of dragooning only Negro children past the local school on their street to shift for their education in schools afar off, and faced with the cost and logistics of such displaced school populations, it might be better for us, after all, to turn back from such onerous external changes, and go for internal changes.

The predominantly Chinese schools in the heart of Boston, with their crack regiments of scholars, or the predominantly corpse-colored, Yankee schools of Wellesley, with their tolerable scholars, feel no loss of hope and prospect by reason of their scholars' studying desk to desk beside only their own kin and kind.

Would it not be better to plant the road to a rewarded future so firmly in the minds of our Negro elementary school schildren in their present, specially-instructed neighborhood schools that they can proceed into racially well diversified Junior High and High School with every sense of the worth of themselves and confidence in their competence to meet life's problems?

Rather than attempt external shifts and transportational changes, resented by Negro parents, would it not be better to give our Negro pupils a change of heart?

And that is exactly what the Boston Schools in their enormous and uncrumpling devotion to their Negro pupils are trying to do.

Edward W. Brooke, the first elected Negro attorney general in the United States, says:

"This is the greatest country in the world for Negroes, and anyone who says it isn't true just doesn't know what he's talking about.

"A lot has got to be done by the Negro himself—by accepting his own responsibilities.

"I think that a man must be judged on his own merit, and I think the Negro must peddle his wares in the marketplace of the world, and be judged by the standards of all mankind.

"I am very pleased to see organizations such as the National Association for the Advancement of Colored People setting up self-help programs.

"I believe very strongly in self-help. Otherwise, you make parasites of people. Sometimes if you have too many crutches, you will never learn to walk. But I recognize that there are some things people cannot do for themselves. I applaud the civil-rights law."

The Boston School Committee, then, will or should continue to keep doors open, through heartening and enriching courses in Negro neighborhood elementary schools. It can or should keep a door open through its Optional Pupil Transfer Policy for Negro elementary school pupils to go to any unfilled elementary school in the city, facilitated by the introduction of free carfares for all elementary school kids. And it could keep doors open to Junior High Schools set only in the presently cosmopolitan white residential territories of our town.

BOSTON PUBLIC SCHOOLS
SCHOOL COMMITTEE
15 BEACON STREET, BOSTON 8, MASSACHUSETTS

ATTORNEY
THOMAS S. EISENSTADT
MEMBER

A careful investigation of the facts pertaining to the discharge of Mr. Jonathan Kozol reveal that the administration of the Boston Public Schools were fully justified in terminating his service.

Contrary to publicized reports, I have found that the poem incident was not the sole reason for Mr. Kozol's discharge. Rather, this particular incident was merely the climax to a series of incidents involving this teacher. On numerous occasions during his six months of service . . . Mr. Kozol was advised and counseled by his Principal, Miss ——, and his Supervisor, Mr. ——, to restrict his reading and reference materials to the list of approved publications. These admonitions were brought about by Mr. Kozol's continual deviation from the 4th grade course of study.

It has been established as a fact that Mr. Kozol taught the poem, "Ballad of the Landlord" to his class and later distributed mimeographed copies of it to his pupils for home memorization. It is also true that a parent of one of the pupils registered a strong objection to the poem to the school principal. Miss ——, properly carrying out her responsibility to all of the pupils and to their parents, admonished the neophyte teacher for his persistent deviation from the course of study. She further suggested that the poem "Ballad of the Landlord" was unsuitable for 4th graders since it could be interpreted as advocating defiance of authority. At this point Mr. Kozol became rude and told Miss ——

that he was a better judge of good literature than she.

The confirmation of the above facts is adequate justification for the discharge of a temporary teacher hired on a day-to-day trial basis. It has been stated quite adequately that the curriculum of this particular school, which is saturated with compensatory programs in an effort to specially assist disadvantaged pupils, does allow for innovation and creative teaching. However, this flexibility does not and should not allow for a teacher to implant in the minds of young children any and all ideas. Obviously, a measure of control over the course of study is essential to protect the 94,000 Boston school children from ideologies and concepts not acceptable to our way of life. Without any restrictions, what guarantees would parents have that their children were not being taught that Adolf Hitler and Nazism were right for Germany and beneficial to mankind?

It should be understood that the fact of the poem's author [sic] happened to be a Negro had no bearing on this matter whatsoever. As a matter of fact, Mr. Kozol was asked by the school principal why other works of Langston Hughes, non-controversial in nature, were not selected for study. In fact, a reference source suggested in the course of study recommends use of the book entitled, "Time for Poetry," published by Foresman which contains six of Langston Hughes' poems; and the Administrative Library contains the book, "More Silver Pennies," by MacMillian [sic] which includes more of Langston Hughes' poems, and also poems by the Negro poet Countee Cullen.

When Miss —— reported the incident to Deputy Superintendent Sullivan and requested Mr. Kozol's removal from the teaching staff of the —— School, it climaxed a series of complaints made to Miss Sullivan's office concerning this particular teacher. Superintendent Ohrenberger's decision after carefully weighing the facts of the case was to relieve Mr. Kozol from further service in the Boston Public Schools.

It should be understood that many temporary teachers are released from service every year by the admin-

istration of the Boston Public Schools. They are released for a variety of reasons. The overwhelming
majority of such cases are discharged because in the
opinion of the administrators and supervisors the certain temporary teachers are found unsuitable in training, personality, or character. Mr. Kozol, or anyone else
who lacks the personal discipline to abide by rules and
regulations, as we all must in our civilized society, is
obviously unsuited for the highly responsible profession
of teaching.

In conclusion, I must add that Mr. Kozol did bring to
his pupils an enthusiastic spirit, a high degree of initiative, and other fine qualities found in the best teachers.
It is my hope that Mr. Kozol will develop his latent
talents and concomitantly develop an understanding
and respect for the value of working within the acceptable codes of behavior.

FROM THE BOSTON *GLOBE*,
JUNE 29, 1965

To THE EDITOR—For someone new to the Boston public school system, Jonathan Kozol showed remarkable brilliance and insight, for he quickly found the fourth grade course of study grossly inadequate.

After all, it was only the product of the Boston teachers themselves. It likely didn't take too long to patch the thing together, although the dull, incompetent workers who labored on it had to pool centuries of collective teaching experience and innumerable hours of unpaid, unpublicized work to get the job finally done.

Lucky for us that someone discovered the fraud. If we're even luckier, maybe the forthright Rhodes scholar will have a new one ready for us when school reopens in the Fall. I certainly hope so.

The Globe's "Talent Go Home" editorial suggests that the school system has been impoverished by the removal of Kozol. Since we are now so bereft, may I suggest that he replace the teachers in the prayers of the poor, deluded parents who until now thought thankfully that their youngsters were in competent, interested hands.

I imagine that Boston's befuddled teachers are dazzled by the recent pyrotechnics in their midst. They know too well how showy, flashy, brief and dangerous these things can be. If they are not all fired during the Summer, we may likely find them again in September, bumbling along the road, carrying little lamps of self-sacrifice, patience and understanding.

They, like myself and the beleaguered administrators, need the Summer off to think up more excuses for the harm we've done.

Me? O, I'm one of the Boston teachers who can't stand to see my system get a knife in the back. Even clods get angry when at home.

ALEXANDER D. VISSER
Hyde Park

FROM THE BOSTON *GLOBE*,
JULY 9, 1965

To THE EDITOR—Reading The Globe letters on the Jonathan Kozol affair, I am struck by an irony he himself has articulated in the past.

George Washington Carver (three times) and Booker T. Washington (twice) have been offered up by correspondents to your letter columns as moral exemplars and inspirational models more appropriate to the developing imaginations of our Negro children than Langston Hughes and his company of "troublemakers."

Now Carver and Washington were estimable men. But it's not an accident that they are the only Negroes receiving honorable mention in standard American history texts.

They were not troublemakers; they do not make us feel guilty. Nor is it an accident that they both lived out their lives at Tuskegee, until just recently a black reservation safely separate from our lives and thoughts.

Nor is it an accident that Globe correspondents distressed by Mr. Kozol's teaching techniques should resort to Carver-Washington as a definition of Negro social acceptability.

From a solution of his forefathers' let blood and slave-sweat, Carver formed a forgiving and beneficent crystal: the peanut. And stored his uncashed paychecks in a shoe box.

Washington left the plantation, went to night school, built Tuskegee, founded the National Negro Business League, and wrote books like "Working with the Hands" and "Putting the Most into Life."

Such defanged respectability is reassuring. It sustains us in our racial reverie. A sort of sociological Muzak, it lulls and comforts us. If only, it whispers, the American Negro would work hard, like the Irish, the Italians, the Swedes: then he, too, would win his slice of the American pie.

No matter that the Irish, the Italians, and the Swedes

came here of their own accord, were given the franchise and permitted the sanctity of the family unit, are not black.

No matter that Federal troops are required to integrate our Southern universities, that white ministers must be murdered to shame us, that Louise Day Hicks out-polls every other candidate for the Boston School Committee.

No matter that the vision of life conspired at by our school primers and our illustrated magazines—a vision into which the gentle botanist may be so effortlessly inserted; a vision cut to the shape of a suburban valentine, populated by station wagons, bicycles, briefcases, cookie jars, dogs, lawns, and electric ranges—is incomprehensible to the urban Negro child.

It bears as little relationship, possesses as little relevance to the world he must live in outside the classroom as science fiction fantasies or Icelandic legends.

No matter, even, that the vision may be a destructive lie for us as well as him, requiring psychiatrists to make us believe in its reality, and soldiers to relieve us of the violence of our frustrations.

No matter. On the Booker T. Washington Memorial at Tuskegee Institute, these words are inscribed: "He lifted the veil of ignorance from his people and found the way to progress through education and industry." From his people . . . and he died fifty years ago.

So trundle him out on casters and present him to fourth-graders: the Good Darkie as Psychic Scare-Crow. Some day, if they're lucky, a few of those fourth-graders may get into Tuskegee. Getting out is tougher. We would much prefer they stay in their place.

JOHN LEONARD
Brighton

BALLAD OF THE LANDLORD

BY LANGSTON HUGHES

Landlord, landlord,
My roof has sprung a leak.
Don't you 'member I told you about it
Way last week?

Landlord, landlord,
These steps is broken down.
When you come up yourself
It's a wonder you don't fall down.

Ten bucks you say I owe you?
Ten bucks you say is due?
Well, that's ten bucks more'n I'll pay you
Till you fix this house up new.

What? You gonna get eviction orders?
You gonna cut off my heat?
You gonna take my furniture and
Throw it in the street?

Um-huh! You talking high and mighty.
Talk on—till you get through.
You ain't gonna be able to say a word
If I land my fist on you.

Police! Police!
Come and get this man!
He's trying to ruin the government
and overturn the land!

Copper's whistle!
Patrol bell!
Arrest.

Precinct station.
Iron cell.
Headlines in press:

MAN THREATENS LANDLORD

TENANT HELD NO BAIL

JUDGE GIVES NEGRO 90 DAYS IN COUNTY JAIL

NOTES

9 Statement of Thomas Eisenstadt presented to Boston parents and press, July 28, 1965.

10 Marguerite Sullivan quoted in Boston *Globe*, Oct. 4, 1964.

10 Boston "Teachers' Handbook," School Document Number One, 1961. See pages 18 and 19.

13 For Boston's loss of two million dollars in Federal aid for compensatory education, see the extensive study of the Boston school system written by W. J. McCarthy and Ronald Kessler and published by the Boston *Herald* over the course of several weeks in the spring of 1966. From the *Herald* of April 14, 1966: "Refusal of school officials to correct deficiencies in Boston's compensatory education program last year cost the city two million dollars. The Office of Economic Opportunity . . . rejected a request by the school department for $2 million in federal funds for Operation Counterpoise because the program was not considered to be compensatory education."

The *Herald* series, a hard-hitting and effective piece of journalism, was not relied upon in this writing due to the fact that its appearance post-dated almost all of the events described and discussed. It provides, however, significant documentation for many of the things that I have said.

35, 36 Boston *Globe*, Dec. 13, 1964.

Boston Municipal Bureau "Special Report," Oct. 1965.

Boston *Globe*, Feb. 9, 1965.

39 Documentation for numbers of unplaced special students is contained in figures submitted by the Superintendent's office to the Mass. State Advisory Committee to the U.S. Commission on Civil Rights, published in its "Report on Racial Imbalance in the Boston Public Schools," January, 1965. See page 32.

51 Boston *Globe*, Dec. 13-18, 1964.

51 Variance in reading levels between predominantly white and predominantly Negro schools is confirmed in the above cited "Report on Racial Imbalance in the Boston Public Schools," based upon figures supplied by the School Department. See page 33.

51, 52 "Interim Report," Advisory Committee on Racial Imbalance and Education, Mass. State Board of Education, July 1, 1964.

53 Boston *Globe,* Jan. 12, 1965.

Since the original writing of this book, Negro parents in Roxbury have instituted and successfully carried out a private bussing program to take advantage of "Open Enrollment." The plan has been successful because of brilliant leadership and organization and because of very heavy support from the suburbs and from some of the foundations. Without outside support, the Roxbury community, for all its courage and imagination, could not maintain the expense of private bussing. The plan, known as Exodus, was transporting about 900 Negro children into white schools as of early 1967. This still left something over 17,000 children in segregated schools.

54 "Interim Report," See pages A-4 and A-5.

54, 55 Report of M. L. Stackhouse presented in lecture and mimeographed form to members of the Harvard Divinity School, February 20 and 21, 1964. The three heavily Negro districts referred to are Garrison, Higginson and Howe. Stackhouse figures are based on research of the Massachusetts Chapter, Americans for Democratic Action and of the Boston Branch, NAACP. The NAACP material is contained in a press statement of June 18, 1963. The A.D.A. material appears in a statement of September 20, 1963.

61 Boston *Globe,* Jan. 18, 1964.

62 *Great Names in American History,* by Gilmartin and Skehan; Laidlaw, 1955.
Famous Men in American History, by Reynolds, Horn and Mizell; Noble and Noble, 1953.
Famous Women, by Wanamaker; Noble and Noble, 1949.
Heroes, Heroines and Holidays, by Thomas and Kelty; Ginn, 1947.

62, 63 *Neighbors Around The World,* by Smith and Sorenson; John C. Winston, 1947, 1952, 1959. See page 156.

63, 64 *Our America,* by Townsend; Allyn and Bacon, 1953. See pages 131, 135, 141.

64 Figures on racial imbalance in the Garrison School, "Interim Report." See page A-4.

69 ff. *Our Neighbors Near and Far*, by Carpenter; American Book Company, 1933. See pages 79, 80, 111, 116, 120, 129, 196.

73, 74 *Journeys Through Many Lands*, by Stull and Hatch; Allyn and Bacon, 1952. This book has been removed from display at the Boston School Committee Library. The publisher, however, has supplied me with a copy of the edition that was in use within my school. For description of the pygmies, see page 79:

"The little people are very good to us when they learn that we do not mean to harm them. They listen with great interest to our small radio, which seems like magic to them. They even give one of their strange dances for us . . . Round and round the little people circle, up and down they jump, backward and forward they bend their almost naked bodies, making funny faces and patting their stomachs. After about an hour, they drop to the ground, tired out."

This book was still being used in Boston up to as late as 1965.

75, 76 *Our World Today*, by Stull and Hatch; Allyn and Bacon, 1955. See pages 9, 95, 120 and 122.

79 *New Streets and Roads*, by Gray, Monroe, Artley and Arbuthnot; Scott, Foresman, 1956. See page 67 ff.

82 *New Streets and Roads*. See page 307 ff.

83 *Stories From Near and Far*, by Orr, Read and Franseth; Scribner's, 1951. See page 83.

84 *Mary Jane*, by Dorothy Sterling; Scholastic Book Services, 1964.

85 *Martin Luther King: The Peaceful Warrior*, by Ed Clayton; Prentice-Hall, 1964.

93 Supt. Ohrenberger is quoted in Boston *Globe*, Jan. 20, 1964.

100, 101 Boston *Globe*, Jan. 6, 1965.
Boston *Globe*, Feb. 21, 1965.

102 I refer to Superintendent Ohrenberger as a "good-hearted football coach." This is a large part of his public reputation. In actuality he has been a math teacher—from 1927 to 1945—although at the same time and during the same years he attracted more attention to himself as a football coach and, apparently, as a general "nice guy." He was, next, administrator of physical education for almost ten years,

after which, it seems, he worked at School Committee headquarters downtown. He holds an unearned doctoral degree from Calvin Coolidge College. At the time that he was chosen Superintendent, the Harvard Education School consultant, Dr. Herold Hunt, had recommended six candidates from outside of Boston ahead of him. Three months before his appointment in September of 1963, Ohrenberger made this promise: "If I'm named superintendent, I'm going to surround myself with real pros." The *Christian Science Monitor* of August 3, 1960, indicates that Ohrenberger actively seems to have sought the job. The *Monitor* of July 14, 1960, makes it clear that he had considerable political pressure building up behind him. Previous to his appointment as Superintendent of Schools, Ohrenberger in 1954 had been put in charge of revising the Boston school curriculum during the course of just one summer: an astonishing job for just one man. He also was involved in a hassle in 1959 over an attempt to get himself a double salary (i.e., his old one and his new one) for the summer months after he had been awarded a promotion. The court ruled against granting Ohrenberger this double salary which he had asked for, according to the Boston *Globe* of December 7, 1959. He finally received appointment as Superintendent, with the backing of Mrs. Hicks, in 1963. A Boston *Globe* clipping, from July 13, 1954, describes him under the sub-heading "Tops as Toastmaster." The piece reads in part: "Ohrenberger is a national figure in the sports world. He has officiated at numerous major collegiate and professional sports events. His reputation as a toastmaster may not be national, but certainly can claim a major infiltration over New England . . . He was adviser and commissioner of the Catholic Youth Organization in 1951, and from 1932 to 1947 was on Boston College's athletic board . . . He was varsity line coach for Boston College football in 1931. Ohrenberger was a member of the Massachusetts Advisory Committee on Service to Youth from 1948 to 1950." Within the terms of Boston, of our schools and colleges, athletics and politics, he has been a great success. In a sense he seems a typical prize-winning product of the kinds of schools he now runs. The only question is whether such a man, shaped by such a system and delimited by it, can find the scope to revitalize it and the intellect to give it new meaning. Seeing him and hearing him that night, it was difficult to believe he could.

123 Boston *Herald*, March 14, 1965.

Boston *Herald*, March 13, 1965.

126 *Record American*, March 16, 1965.

136, 137 "Report of the Advisory Committee on Racial Imbalance and Education," Mass. State Board of Education, April, 1965. See page 2.

137, 138 Boston *Globe*, April 15, 1965.

Boston *Globe*, April 16, 1965.

Boston *Herald*, April 16, 1965.

141, 142 Boston *Globe*, April 23, 1965.

143 Boston *Globe*, March 18, 1965.

143 Boston *Globe*, April 19, 1965. Statements quoted from the Easter Sermon of Rev. Wilbur Ziegler and confirmed by Rev. Caldwell.

144 ff. Boston *Globe*, April 5, 1965.

Boston *Globe*, April 9, 1965. The pay-raise for the Superintendent and others was stalled in the final event for budgetary reasons. It was not rescinded, however, and they received it beginning in the following year.

147 Boston *Globe*, May 27, 1965.

147, 148 Boston *Globe*, April 26, 1965.

Boston *Globe*, June 1, 1965.

Boston *Herald*, April 26, 1965.

Record American, April 26, 1965.

167 *Wide Doors Open*, by Sloop, Garrison and Creekmore; The Economy Company, 1954.

173 *SRA Reading Laboratory, IIa*, by Don W. Parker; Science Research Associates Inc., 1958.

173 ff. "A Curriculum Guide, Elementary Education, Grades IV-V-VI," A Publication of the Boston Public Schools, Document Number 7, 1959. See pages 9, 52, 76 and 77.

179 ff. "Curriculum Guide in Character Education," School Document Number 11, 1962. See pages 6, 7, 8, 9, 15, 16, 48 and 49.

184, 185 For attitudes of school officials regarding the background of the Negro children, see the quotation from Mrs. Hicks, Boston *Herald*, January 17, 1965. See also statement of Dr. Frederick J. Gillis, Superintendent of the Boston Public Schools, 1960 to 1963, quoted in the "Report on Racial Imbalance in the Boston Public Schools," pages 59 and 60.

185 Miss Sullivan quoted in her report on "Operation Counter-Poise"—Henry L. Higginson District, 1963-1964. See page 6.

186 *Coming of Age in America,* by Edgar Z. Friedenberg; Random House, 1965. See pages 242 and 243.

194 ff. The poems of Langston Hughes referred to are "Madam And Her Madam," "Merry-Go-Round" and "Ballad of the Landlord." See *Selected Poems of Langston Hughes,* Alfred A. Knopf, 1959.

200 Quotations from the Principal are taken from her letter of June 14, 1965, to Miss Marguerite Sullivan, Deputy Superintendent, Boston Public Schools, as it has been placed in my permanent School Department record.

204, 205 Mr. Ohrenberger quoted in Boston *Herald,* June 12, 1965.

Miss Sullivan quoted in Boston *Herald,* June 13, 1965, and *Christian Science Monitor,* June 19, 1965.

School employee quoted anonymously in Boston *Herald,* June 13, 1965.

207 Mr. Eisenstadt quoted in Boston *Traveler,* June 17, 1965, and Boston *Globe,* June 17, 1965.

212, 213 For Mr. Eisenstadt's upholding of my dismissal see his complete report as appended to this book.